ORDINARY THINGS

ORDINARY THINGS

A DIFFERENT KIND OF VOYAGE

Christopher PRATT

EDITED AND WITH A FOREWORD BY
TOM HENIHAN

BREAKWATER

LIBRARY AND ARCHIVES CANADA CATALOGUING IN PUBLICATION

Pratt, Christopher, 1935-
Ordinary things : a different kind of voyage / Christopher Pratt.
ISBN 978-1-55081-264-0
1. Pratt, Christopher, 1935- --Diaries.
2. Painters--Canada--Diaries. 3. Newfoundland and Labrador--Biography.
I. Title.
ND249.P7A2 2009   759.11   C2009-902808-5

Editor: Tom Henihan
All images from the author's personal collection, except as noted
Author photograph: Ned Pratt
Cover image Collection RBC Financial Group

ॐ

BREAKWATER BOOKS LTD. acknowledges the support of the Canada Council for the Arts
which last year invested $20.1 million in writing and publishing throughout Canada.
We acknowledge the financial support of the Government of Canada through the Book
Publishing Industry Development Program for our publishing activities. We acknowledge
the financial support of the Government of Newfoundland and Labrador through the
department of Tourism, Culture and Recreation for our publishing activities.

Printed in Canada

Canada Council Conseil des Arts   Canada   Newfoundland
for the Arts   du Canada   Labrador

ENVIRONMENTAL BENEFITS STATEMENT

Breakwater Books Ltd. saved the following
resources by printing the pages of this book on
chlorine free paper made with 100% post-consumer
waste.

TREES	WATER	SOLID WASTE	GREENHOUSE GASES
11	5,189	315	1,077
FULLY GROWN	GALLONS	POUNDS	POUNDS

Calculations based on research by Environmental Defense and the Paper Task Force.
Manufactured at Friesens Corporation

ACKNOWLEDGEMENTS

I AM indebted to Breakwater Books, especially Rebecca Rose, Clyde Rose, Annamarie Beckel and Anna Kate MacDonald, for their support and enthusiasm for this project. It originates from many years of notes, diaries, boat logs, and car books, skipping along their surfaces like a stone on a rippled pond, avoiding – for now – its depths. Rhonda Molloy brought her own understanding of St. Mary's Bay to its design and layout; Chad Pelley has been entirely respectful of the voice and origins of these often-rambling entries. They have all been very responsive to my concerns and objectives, and effective in their realization.

My thanks to poet and editor, Tom Henihan, whom I first met when he edited *A Painter's Poems*, for his guidance in the selection of material included here from a much wider, but necessarily limited base, and for the counsel, sensitivity, and advice he brought to the process of adjusting the language of the diary for a wider audience, while preserving its voice and respecting its codes.

My secretary, Brenda Kielley, has exhibited characteristic patience and professionalism throughout what seemed to be endless adjustments and changes. My children, John, Anne, Barbara, and Ned, and my brother Philip, continue to meet me with care, humour, and forbearance. Many friends and colleagues, in particular the poet Tom Dawe, Tom Smart, Director of the McMichael Canadian Art Collection, and Mira Godard and Gisella Giacalone at The Mira Godard Gallery, have been helpful, encouraging, generous in their understanding, and wise in their 'cautionary verse.' Nor do I forget the profound contribution Mary West Pratt has brought to my work and my life.

My wife and assistant, Jeanette Meehan Pratt, gallantly takes the blame for every bump and pothole in the road that jars my hand as I write, while she drives, and we go in search of this wonderful province – much of it already familiar to me, most of it new to her. Her company and enthusiasm enriches all of it.

I have always been surrounded by tolerant, intelligent, caring and compassionate people – friends and family alike. I thank them all, many now, sadly, in absentia. They inhabit this book at its centre, or just off stage. It is dedicated to them, and in particular to my parents, Emily Christina Dawe and John Kerr Pratt, who were known to their friends, ordinarily, as 'Chris and Jack.'

Christopher Pratt
July 7, 2009
Salmonier

FOREWORD

CHRISTOPHER PRATT has written all of his life, marking the ordinary days and events of his life, and those framed by special significance and circumstance. Whether he is writing on a matter of obvious importance or something apparently less decisive, everything is afforded the same consideration. This is consistent with the inherent belief, expressed in a number of different contexts in this book, that the significance things have is the significance we bring to them. In a piece written in 1975, he speaks about his own early awareness in this regard, "I believed that picturesque, photogenic, beautiful or even magnificently ugly things had no more claim to precedent than the unadorned, unlit cupboard door outside my bedroom. The sun, a mighty presence, had no greater reality than the 40-watt bulb whose terrestrial energy it had ordained." He finishes the piece by saying, "In the face of it, all things are equal in the fact that they exist."

This book is composed of pieces from journals and diaries written from the 1950s to the present, covering a broad spectrum of subject matter and a variety of genres: travel pieces, epigram, humorous anecdote, prose poems. But it is not fragmentary – an undertaking as important as his 2005 retrospective, the triumphs and frustrations of a painter's life, sailing from Lake Ontario to Conception Bay, Newfoundland, time spent with family and friends, hiking in the Tablelands, or sitting alone on the deck at night at his home in Salmonier, are all rendered as integral aspects of a single picture. While the pieces in this book constitute the story of a life, it is neither autobiography nor memoir, but more accurately, as Christopher Pratt himself has described it, a self-portrait.

Tom Henihan, 2008

PROLOGUE

I HAVE always had a sense that there is an immense presence in ordinariness. This ordinariness is not a celebration of the sordid or the tawdry or the trite: it celebrates the non-exotic, the anti-picturesque. Conceptually, it is totally North American: it is Hopper's hotel rooms and Hemingway's descriptions of Nick Adams and Alex Colville's cows. It is that substrate of self-consciousness and insecurity that troubles the surface bravado of Walt Whitman's poetry; it is Grant Wood's innocence in offering *American Gothic* up to ridicule. It is why Mary Cassatt ought not to have gone to Paris and why Georgia O'Keefe and Emily Carr did better staying home. It is the difference in the albeit mannered peopling of paintings by Thomas Hart Benton and the peasants in the work of Jean Francois Millet – who still owed much to Maccicio. It is Shaker furniture, but it is never puritanical. It is the dignity of things that have nothing going for them beyond the fact of their existence. It is an ordinariness saturated with democracy, with potential, like the hum you hear in a length of rope stretched to its limit, just before it breaks.

MY APPENDIX abandoned me at the Grace Hospital in St. John's on Thursday, July 17, 1952, Dr. Harry Roberts presiding. That was the summer I graduated from Prince of Wales College.

I had a string of encounters with what we then called 'summer complaint.' My mother, who had 'seen a lot' as a nurse in Montreal and St. John's, got nervous about my symptoms so she and Harry decided that it was better to be safe than sorry. As a result, I had the surgery and spent much of that summer convalescing in our back garden on Waterford Bridge Road while my buddies were off trouting, swimming, courting ...

In 2004, fifty-two years later, my cousin Jamie Puddester entrusted to me our grandfather J.C. Pratt's diaries. They had come to him following the death of his mother Gwenyth, my father's older sister, in 2003. Grandfather Jim's diaries are as brief as mine are rambling. His entries for that and subsequent days are as follows:

> *Thursday, July 17th – S.W. Dull and warm.*
> *Christopher operated on today for appendicitis. Doing well, so far.*
> *Ned Foran's brother killed today in fall from roof of Belvedere Orphanage.*
> *"Nothing in life is to be feared. It is only to be understood."*
> *Madame Curie.*
>
> *Saturday, July 19th – N.E. Cloudy and cool – cleared about 11:00 a.m. Fine and warm.*
> *Jack gone with Chester for a week's cruise on his boat.*
> *At the office till noon, but came home feeling sick.*
>
> *Thursday, July 24th – West. Fine – very warm.*
> *Temperature's 82° in the shade. Uncomfortably hot.*
> *Christopher not very well today.*

Saturday, July 26th – N.W. Fine and cool in the morning.
Adlai Stevenson nominated democratic candidate for USA
last night.
Christopher home from the hospital.
Drove across the Marine Drive and out the Portugal Cove
Road to Broadcove Road. Painting in backyard this
afternoon. Very warm.
Minnie, Daphne and Floss at Gwenyth's for tea.
Called at Jack's with book on watercolour painting for
Christopher, who seems much better.

I still have the book, *Water Color Painting* by Adolf Dehn, in my studio.

Mom went to the stationery department at Ayre's on Water Street and bought me a set of paints and brushes. I had seen the sets of watercolours in the brightly lit showcase beneath the glass counter. They were individually wrapped in enameled boxes, flanked by needle-pointed brushes, like spears with black lacquered handles, shining against the matte white sheet of watercolour paper they lay on. They were stocked on the advice of a 'daughter of the house,' Agnes M. Ayre, whose ambition it was to illustrate all the wildflowers of Newfoundland. My mother had an eye for quality as well, so I began what was to become a passion and a career with Winsor & Newton watercolours and Series 7 sable brushes.

James Charles Spurgeon Pratt,
c. 1905-1910

September 1953
Letters Home from Mt. Allison

I was in to see Mr. Harris today. He asked me if I knew Mr. Goodrich and when I said I had met him once, he appeared interested. He offered to arrange a special landscape course for me, at no extra cost. I told him I painted in watercolours, but would like to learn oils. I told him how I have been using watercolours, and about how 'critics' say it's unorthodox. He said, "You forget the critics." He even suggested I take fine arts but, of course, I told him that was definitely out, that art mustn't interfere with my pre-med. He assured me it wouldn't.

Anyway, I can paint what my heart desires whatever way I like. He's even going to have an instructor watch me personally. He's very anxious to see my work, says it's quite important, so I would like you to send some of the recent things, plus Aunt Phyl's and the one in Sonia's room.

The course costs $48.00. Paints, brushes, etc. are extra, but I really think it's worthwhile. After all, $48.00 is only one good picture.

October 9, 1953

I must be frank, I suppose, since it's your only way of knowing. As soon as Mr. Harris saw my watercolour, *Outline*, he called the other teachers off the job and into a powwow. Apparently, he believes I have talent. He said, "I was in Newfoundland last year to pick pictures for the Canadian Exhibition. I knew no one, but was introduced to Goodrich and Shepherd. Nobody told me about you." When I told him I hadn't started painting then – well Mom, he just thinks I should drop everything else. He and the group of people he asked in said things which I never dreamed existed. I pointed out my crudeness in using opaque whites and blacks, etc. He said he wouldn't mind if I used toothpaste and shoe polish.

I was flabbergasted. Well, it's Thanksgiving weekend, and I'm not going anywhere – I was asked, mind you, but Roland Thornhill is coming up tomorrow.

Summer 1954
Excerpts from a notebook I kept when I worked as a warden on
Piper's Hole River, at Swift Current, Placentia Bay, after my
first year at Mt. Allison. I was eighteen at the time.

Sunday, June 20, 1954 Wind S.W.

Arrived at Swift Current to await P.J. Bannister, fisheries officer.
River two inches above normal – no salmon or trout but both
outside – caught in the nets. Hot and fine all day. Moved into
shack – what a shack! If the flies don't eat me, or the stove smoke
too much, I'll live. Put up new screens. There's no glass in the
windows! Got stored away; built wood horse, etc. The kettle is
on now. I need a wash.

I had a look but, alas – no outhouse and no well. I'll have to build
the outhouse, but I'll be damned if I'll dig a well. I'll drink from
the river.

Thursday, June 24, 1954

Today was very fine and hot, but with cloudy patches. It did rain
last night, but not very much. The river is down to 00 inches. It
was 0 + 1/2 this a.m. Walked up to Mother's Brook today – up
to the first of the steadies.

Wired Dad today – still no word on the bike or battery radio, or
my marks from Mt. A. Salmon are reported at Come by Chance,
and a few have been seen in the arm here. There are none in the
river yet. The wind is S, it may rain tonight but I doubt it.

Friday, June 25, 1954

Well it looks like I'll walk or hitch all summer. It was overcast all
day but no rain. Wind South. Not a sign of a fish. Don and Judy
Hollett stopped in on their way to town tonight.

Sunday, June 27, 1954

Rained hard last night, water rose 1 foot, 1 inch. I noticed the following: it stopped raining at eight. Shortly after the river was at 0 + 8 inches. However, it continued to rise to 0 + 13 inches. Dad and Pete arrived in the evening, bringing Pete's old Raleigh bike for me.

No fish around. I hear that the caplin are in the bay, so it won't be long now. It was overcast all day – loads of flies. Remodeled furniture to make a toilet – I cut a round hole in the seat of an 'antique' kitchen chair! I'll lug it into the woods with me.

July 7, 1954

Caught first salmon this morning. It was a miserable 3½-pound excuse for a fish. I caught it right where I hooked a fish yesterday. Eugene Beck hooked three in the same spot, all larger, but didn't land any of them. Weather was so-so. I have two fellas – Bern Goobie and Pete – here tonight, so I have lots of company.

July 12, 1954

Orangemen's Day: The Glorious 12th of July … six Girl Guides staying in a cabin on Otter Rub Brook – hundred yards upstream. I'll have to keep an eye on them. I'm afraid they may be hauling the river …

Warden's cabin at Piper's Hole River, 1954

Fall 1955
Letters Home from Mt. Allison

I've been doing a bit of writing lately and some colour sketches of the marshes. I don't expect I'll do much more than sketch, but that keeps me in touch. Mary and I always study the exhibitions in the Art Gallery and take notes on them.

In my English courses, especially modern poetry, I find my ideas and the professor's seem to get along better this year.

It's the hunting season and you see deer draped over pickup fenders going through town every day now. They're very small; I'm told a 250-pound buck was shot in N.S., but 150 pounds is considered big. I was hunting one afternoon last week. The country here is all farm land; small birch groves and hedgerows. We were hunting pheasants but it was too wet. We went out on the marshes later and Johnny Bursey (a buddy of mine from Gander) shot a teal.

It's hard to realize that I haven't been home in the fall for three years now. I've missed a lot of painting. The sea, the barrens, everything is much more intense then, and I like that. I don't mean the 'theatrical' colours; it's the sharp, cold colours and lines, the dark blue days, and the bare weather of oncoming winter that I like.

Mary West and Christopher Pratt at Sackville, 1955

June 27, 1957
Southeast Placentia

I've been working on the Base for a month now. I didn't like it at first, but I soon got used to it. I like the Yanks. They're good to work with. They can be condescending but they're ok if you give them as good as you get. They like that.

I started out as a rod man. But Larry Fahey knew I had done surveying at Memorial in '52-'53, so he got me set up as an instrument man. Thanks to that and Roger Crosbie, my pay went from $35 to $75 a week. We're on the job by 7:00 a.m. and I often don't get back to the cabin until 9:00 p.m. or later. I don't mind having no electricity, running water or telephone. Mom will bring out the mail when they come for the weekend, so if there's a letter from Mary (there's been one a week) it will arrive then. I haven't written her as often as I should. I get pretty tired, as this late night scrawl by lamplight will attest.

My privacy will be shattered when they get here, and I will be restless until they leave. I feel badly about that.

Southeast River

1957
Southeast Placentia

I finished work on the Base and got my final cheque from Ayers Hagen Booth last week, but I'm back at the cabin for a few days. We hardly got fishing all summer so Kevin, Bernard and I are going to take advantage of next Monday being Labour Day, take the tent and hike across the country to Barachois. Arthur O'Keefe says our best bet is to leave the road at the Six Mile and follow the trail to the Beehive Waters, then cut over and cross Little Salmonier River where it runs out of Brian's Pond. He hasn't been past there in a long time but he remembers it's southwest and across open marshes from there. Dad says there's no need to go 'all the way to the landwash,' because the trout will be up in the headwaters by now anyway. Mom's worried about the amount of time I'll have left to get ready to go to Fredericton, but the stuff I'll be taking to Glasgow is already packed in a steamer trunk to go 'cargo' on the *RMS Nova Scotia* en route Liverpool, the same boat Mary and I will take two days after the wedding.

The cabin at Southeast Placentia, 1960

Letters Home from Glasgow

September 29

We came up from Liverpool to Glasgow on the train Tuesday night. It passed through the Lake District but I didn't see any lakes. It was really beautiful, with sharply defined fields and hedgerows and small stone houses and barns in the hollows. It is very peaceful and terribly ordered. To be frank, I find the degree of order disturbing.

December 15

Whatever my potential as an artist may be, I realize that it doesn't change just because I happen to be living in a place unlike my home. The craft of painting is the same basic thing no matter where it is taught and that is what I am here to learn. The why of painting is something different entirely: it is something that you know or do not know. It is a constant over which there is little control. It may be that no amount of study can bring it where it does not exist, but nothing can destroy it where it does.

February 21

I venture to say that very few people who paint are honest enough to put down what they see, rather than what they think they should see. I have often gone out sketching and come home empty-handed because, subconsciously enough, I had spent the whole time looking for places that resembled pictures I have seen. I was trying to see with someone else's eyes ...

December 6

The worst kind of a day here is represented by a damp, raw, dark, choking smog. How I wish it would blow a decent gale once in a while. Even a good sleet storm would help. You don't realize the beauty of many things until you do not have them: the wonderful feeling when you wake up on a morning when there has been fresh snow, and you know the ground is white before you look out from the brightness of the room, or the stronger light reflected from the snow in the night time ...

March 14

When people who knew anything about painting saw my first efforts in watercolours, the invariable comment was that I should use oils. That was because I used watercolour partially in an opaque manner, which is not the general way of using them. I used to think that I could use the transparent paint for things that were transparent, like water and sky, and that things like rocks would look better if painted more densely and solidly. I still think that, but I meet opposition on all sides at school here; it suggests that since I use opaque areas in watercolours I will have to use transparent areas in oils – and that is frowned upon here even more than the first.

Grosvenor Crescent, Glasgow, 1957

Spring 1959
Excerpts from Letters from My Mother

"Christopher,

... none of this being an artist will come easily for you. You take it all too seriously. Being an artist is no more important or special than being a businessman or a carpenter ... a nurse, a doctor, or a fisherman. It's just another thing that people do. Like everything, some do it better than others, and you will be one of them ... but life is more important than art ... always remember that. And don't talk about 'art' all the time."

Emily Christina Dawe, c.1933

1961
Letters Home from Mt. Allison

February 13

I have completed *Boat in Sand*, the most ambitious thing I have done since I returned from Glasgow to Mt. Allison last year. Mr. Colville thinks it is "a very lovely thing," and Mr. Harris has bought one for $30.00. I have traded one with Mr. Pulford for one of his watercolours.

February 17

Mr. Pulford told me yesterday he felt it was the finest picture that has ever been done here. I'm sure you'll see that this is not a particular boat in a particular place. It is to me a piece of the fishing industry, washed up on a sand beach. There is a lot of 'across-the-bay' in it, and of course, there is a lot of Pt. Lance on the Cape Shore. I think there is a genuine affection for boats.

I don't know what to say about the cabin burning, at least not now. We're a sentimental lot I guess, and there's always a danger of gushing. Still, if this is our weakness it is also a strength that gives us an enjoyment of things many people may not notice. I lived there when I worked on the Base, and it was through the cabin that I came to know aspects of the Cape Shore, desolate and harsh though it may sometimes be. Ever since we have had the cabin, my work has revolved around the Cape Shore. Because of that, and for many less involved things, this will be a great loss.

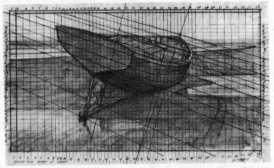

Study for Boat in Sand, 1960

1962
The Extension Service Years

On Teaching at Carbonear

It was a black night, in spite of the full moon. The low, heavy clouds swept in from the sea, their movement just discernible above the rim of the hills. A light showed in the window of a small wooden church. A bell rang, not from the belfry it seemed, but from the hollowness of the church itself, rhythmic yet irregular, the footsteps of a crippled man in an empty corridor. The bell made its appeal to the universe, which has enough space to receive and lose all the appeals that were ever made or ever will be; it went across the land and was absorbed into the darkness. Then the bell faded away and the light went out. What remained was the noise of the sea, and the wind, and an almost imperceptible line between the barrens and the sky.

Some members of the faculty and staff of
Memorial University of Newfoundland Extension Service, 1961-63

Photograph: Frank Kennedy, St. John's Daily News, Courtesy
of Memorial University of Newfoundland and Labrador

August 1963
Salmonier

I anchored the boat in the river after everyone left and did a drawing of the roots of spruce trees where they are undercut along the riverbank. I then went ashore and into the woods and did a drawing of an old, moss-covered birch tree. These are the first drawings I have done since I quit my job with the Extension Service and moved here to live three months ago. We have had hoards of visitors all summer, but that's over now, so I can get at converting 'Gert's cottage' into a studio. Dad sent down a skylight, generously but against his better judgment – he says they always leak. 'Mr. Tom' is going to install it tomorrow, and a space heater later on.

I went fishing on the pond after supper. It was reminiscent of evenings spent on Jim Crowe's Pond ten or fifteen years ago. We used to go there in the spring, and the trout would start to rise at dusk, when the snipe started winnowing. I got half a dozen trout, all of them on a 'Cow Dung' or a 'McGinty.' Brown trout seem to favour flies of their own colour.

John starts school at Our Lady of Mt. Carmel next week. I always imagined my children starting school at Holloway and going on to Prince of Wales. Mary and my parents are concerned, but Mom, having attended an outport school herself, 'rhymes off' at every opportunity a list of many brilliant and accomplished Newfoundlanders who have come from one. And it's not an issue of denomination; I had a frank and friendly talk with the parish priest, Fr. Ed Purcell, about that. Anyway, I have assured them it will only be for a year.

March 1964

I began work today on a serigraph print – an idea based on sheets drying in the spring. I spent the early part of the week enlarging the working drawing from smaller drawings I had made off and on over a period of three or four years. Experimenting with the same drawings two years ago led to the painting *House and Barn*, and in many respects the present work is like it. The proportion and arrangement of the two houses is practically the same; both pictures being laid out in double dynamic-symmetry rectangles. But the print is concerned with a different time of year, with values different from those I was preoccupied with in *House and Barn* that, to me, justify the near repetition of some aspects of the work.

I had begun the year by enlarging and laying out the drawing for an oil painting of *Tessier's Barn*. I had painted in an undercoat, but I decided to abandon the picture, at least temporarily, because there will be opportunities to exhibit prints this spring if the ones I am planning are satisfactory. But, more important, the subjects I have in mind for prints now appeal to me more, perhaps because they have more to do with my present life. The idea for *Tessier's Barn* concerns another time and place with many associations that have meaning for me, but are not as alive in my mind at present as other things that are closer to me now.

The house at Salmonier, 1961

Considering the reviews I have read in the past few days concerning the work of painters from Atlantic Canada, I should find it difficult to muster enough self-confidence and feeling to continue with my work. The critic John Russell, reviewing the Dunn Invitational for *Art News* from London, refers to the Atlantic region as "that distant and inhospitable part of Canada." I presume he meant distant from the mainstream of art, although I can imagine him being ignorant of the fact that New Brunswick is geographically nearer to London than New York is. No doubt, he would consider Newfoundland to be well behind New Brunswick, unless he deems both so inconsequential as to make comparisons ridiculous. Referring to a prize awarded to Alex Colville, Russell says, "Only by an apotheosis of hick taste could his picture have been chosen." Presumably, this is a reference, not only to Colville's realistic method of painting, but also to what is, on the surface, the provincial, backwoods nature of his subject. My subjects would be considered even more provincial than his. I am a realist who cannot draw very well and does not command the mastery of technique necessary to bring to realism that sharp and breathless quality that can be self-sustaining.

In a review of the exhibition New Images from Canada, Diana Armatage writing from New York for *Canadian Art Magazine*, refers to the "dangerous Mt. Allison manner," while conceding that the "Tenth Street manner" is also dangerous. She observes that Mt. Allison's students are too concerned with "making pictures of things, rather than making paintings," as if paintings may not be pictures of things, that the two are eternally separate. She also refers to "the heartless and dulling demands of reproducing exactly either nature or other men's (i.e. Wyeth's) paintings of nature." I am a Mt. Allison realist too.

In a third review, also in *Canadian Art*, David Silcox comments from London on the reaction of the British press to the Fifth Biennial of Canadian Art, shown at the Commonwealth Institute last summer. He makes light of the coverage in what he calls, properly I think, the "large circulation, low mentality dailies" and refers to the reviews in the "astute" papers as "brief, patronizing notices." He quotes as most significant the *Apollo* review, which finishes with the observation that "the sprinkling of what could be called 'traditional' paintings is so bad as to be embarrassing." Presumably, my offering *Woman at a Dresser*, selected for the show by William Townsend, vice-principal of the Slade, was one of, if not the most 'traditional' painting of the group. *Canadian Art Magazine* itself has not reviewed the Fifth Biennial except through reports of its reception in London, perhaps because there is some bad blood between the editors of the magazine and the National Gallery. Maybe the editors wish to align themselves with the international sophistication of the London reaction by inference. Perhaps they consider an exhibition, selected coast to coast with 'Hockey Night in Canada' patriotism, and containing examples of the provincial as well as the metropolitan styles, to be academic in the old sense and damaging to Canada's reputation, and by extension their own, when sent abroad?

Woman at a Dresser, 1964, Oil on board, The McMichael Canadian Art Collection

1965
Dom Ryan's Dory

At the crack of dawn this morning, Philip, Les Tuck and I left Kielley's wharf aboard *Walrus* en route to Big Barachois. We were towing Dom Ryan's dory, which we had borrowed for the day, so we could anchor-off, row ashore and walk around the beach to the river. With the Lister diesel ticking away, we were rolling along into a big, glassy swell running up the bay, when, just about half a mile northwest of Little Colinet Island, we noticed the hawser draw tight. Checking astern, we could see that the dory was starting to swamp and getting low in the water. We handed her in as fast as we could and sure enough the bung had popped out and was bobbing around in the bilge. She started to fill faster as we slowed down and stopped, so Philip had to haul on one of the musty, mildewed life vests, hop aboard and stomp the bung back into its hole. We then motored under the lee of the island and half an hour later had the dory bailed out and were back on course.

Commenting as always on the potential folly of using a five-claw graplen on a sand bottom, we dropped the hook offshore in the middle of the bight, well outside where the swell was breaking on the beach, then rowed ashore. The sun was starting to burn off the mist as we took a shortcut across the dunes and headed up the river, intending to fish at the estuary on our way back. Les could identify every bird we saw or heard – terns and gulls, sparrows and warblers – a great mixed morning chorus. We walked up to the forks, and fished our way down, pool by pool. The river was fresh and clear, bubbling peaty brown, and there were salmon and sea trout everywhere we would expect them to be: the trout in the deeper water, the salmon near the tails of the pools. I fished with a #8 Blue Charm all day, except that I put on a 3" Grey Ghost streamer when we got back to the tidewater, where the salmon won't usually take but the trout are hungry and mistake it for a caplin. We kept a dozen trout and five salmon, each of the latter 4½ pounds: firm, silver, fresh from the sea and as alike as peas in a pod. Les, the naturalist, proposed that they had left the river together as smolt and returned in company to spawn. Back aboard

Walrus, we got the Coleman stove going as we headed out into the bay and the chill of a late afternoon fog. We made hot Nescafe coffee thick with Carnation milk to warm ourselves and wash down the homemade raisin tea biscuits and black currant jam Mary had sent along to sustain us. We rounded Big Barachois and Little Salmonier Points, then set a course for Salmonier Arm, ten miles to the northeast.

I'm not going to tell Dom about the bung, he may think we were careless. He may also think that we were criticizing him for not having it secured, but why would he? The dory was on shore, high and dry. We might need it again.

1965

We were walking on the sand, holding our boots and socks in one hand and a fly rod in the other. The sea – rising, curling, breaking – swept around our ankles like a scythe, cutting, green and frigid, flooding to our knees. It was one of those June days, with the sun burning through a ghost-like mist, a residue of the ancient glacier that carved the bay. Inland, up in the valley past sand dunes capped with tough, bright grass, it would be hot, the bogs as organic as the sand was crystalline. I was talking about all of that, to myself primarily, but also to anybody listening, and one of them said: "Jesus, listen to him will you – thinks he's a fuckin' poet."

We caught a lot of strong, silver trout like living ice: flawless, dappled, iridescent, mimicking the sky. Across the estuary where we fished, at the far end of the beach, there was a boat stranded on the shore. That was in June, 1951. Ten years later, working on *Boat in Sand* at Mt. Allison, I thought of all of that.

1965

Mike Cook came down for supper last night and picked up some things he's going to include in a reading of Newfoundland poetry; he could read the telephone directory and make it sound like Shakespeare. *Night Window*, just finished, is still in my studio and we got talking about it. I am looking out a window into blackness, seeing the reflection of a fireplace and mirror I remember from the flat where I lived as a child. Mike saw that I had consciously left out my own reflection and he asked me why. He said he thought it would be a good format for a self-portrait. I admitted that the self-portrait idea had occurred to me and 'maybe another time.' A night window is a corruption – something meant to admit light and let you see out, becomes a reflection of your room, of what you already know. Does that imply that in reality we can only see what is in ourselves? The devices we employ to give us access to an unknown are illusory, and no matter where we look, we can only find a looking glass.

April 10, 1967

Tonight I tried, yet again, to start a landscape drawing or water-colour of a landscape, but I was unable to. I have grown very far away from that part of my work; I suppose I am being drawn, or led, into a more formal type of painting. It makes me restless. I feel this is because, if I continue doing figure work of this sort, I will have to go where the figures are. I am certainly not preoccupied with the Salmonier landscape. It all seems so dilute by comparison with the human body.

The Tickles, St. Mary's Bay

1967

St. Patrick's Day

Yesterday was quite a day. We woke up to find the water frozen. After I got Mr. Tom organized to fix it, we drove in to town through a bad storm, picked up the Wests and came home again. Later it cleared up a bit and Mary and I went back in to town for her opening, leaving her parents here to look after the children – with Barby brewing a cold. The show was a great success. Today has been stormy. I haven't done much.

March 20, 1967

The Wests leave this morning. We took them to St. John's yesterday and went to see Mary's show again. Five or six more paintings have sold. I feel bad about the way I acted when they were here. I have a short fuse when it comes to Newfoundland and this place in particular, and I take offense where maybe none is intended.

The weather was beautiful today. I suggested setting up a studio in the corner room for Mary but she was hesitant, as usual, to commit herself to that. I suppose I had better forget it and get on with my own work. I still am not decided on what to do next. Bernadette will be home for a week starting Friday, and that will give me a chance to do the drawing for *A Woman Lying Down*. I intended this for the summer, but I am more interested in it than anything else. Since so much time has gone by without getting a start on other things, it's a good idea to get at it now.

January 24, 1968

I started painting the figure today which is a step or two ahead of my previous pace. I have always found my work progressed only after it had reached a stage where corrections and changes, improvements, were implicit in what had already been achieved. The less accomplishment at a given stage, the fewer and narrower the opportunities for extension. As time goes by, I should no longer have to repeat all the 'stages,' hangovers from the hesitation in my earlier work.

January 29, 1968

It rained all day today, and now it is a mild, foggy, musty-smelling night. The water in the river gurgles around the ice, which occasionally cracks or shifts as the river drops and rises. It is very still and there is no noise in the woods; the sort of night you feel you could hear a rabbit run or the small sounds of field mice tunneling under the snow. I always think of the places deep in the country where things change with the forces of nature, unobserved – where ice shifts and waterfalls rumble, softened in the fog and snow. That may seem romantic, but that is how things are happening in the vast, unimaginable universe. It sometimes seems that in the absence of man the world is more a part of the universe: the universe invades it.

I painted frames for Mary today.

With Mary West Pratt, Salmonier River, 1981
Photograph: John Reeves

April 1969

Donna was here for drawing for the first time tonight, but my efforts were not up to par. She is very animated and unselfconscious and could be an exceptional model. She has no pretensions or preconceptions, an ordinary girl with enough self-confidence to get undressed. I have a long way to go before I get anywhere near doing her justice.

In the original studio, 1970
Photograph: John Reeves

May 23, 1970
Cape Shore

Often, in April and May, we went trouting at the mouth of a brook or river where it entered the sea. That was different from fishing inland, where the countryside was wild and tangled with black spruce and juniper, where trout came dark from peat-stained water. At the estuary, everything was silver, bright, and there were measured fields and houses, often abandoned.

I like the marks that cultivation leaves – furrows and edges, the evidence of mankind where our presence is benign. I like places that are barren and exposed, where houses stand unsheltered, where I can taste salt in the air and the light seems to be carried on the wind.

Anne is ten years old today.

1970

I worked all day but it is going nowhere fast. I tried 'taking off' some slides last night, but I can't get enthusiastic about that. When I did the *Young Woman Dressing* painting, I had a very strong drawing to work from; done carefully and over time, directly from life, it defined volumes and surfaces, textures and temperatures. Bernadette's mood changed from day to day as I worked at it and it became a more extensive record than the one-sixtieth of a second click of a camera.

When I was working on the painting itself, I referred to the drawing and the richness it contained. Still, whenever I could, I had Bernadette in the studio though I hardly ever looked at her, except for a glance – the equivalent, perhaps, of that shutter click. But her presence there made the painting possible: her moods, her observations, and her responses. That was always important to me.

1971
Hemmer Jane

The Coast of Labrador

We left Quirpon at daylight and set a course close by the Sacred Islands, then generally north-northwest toward Chateau Bay on the Labrador coast. The forecast was for winds southwest 10 knots increasing to 15 knots around noon, which would get up a good lop if the tide happened to be against it, steep-to and right on our port beam. *The Hemmer Jane* has a flat 'yacht' bottom and only a shallow keel, so she 'rolls somethin' shockin' in those conditions. Of course, we had the option of putting into Henley Harbour for shelter if it came to that. But there was no sign of it; about ten miles south of Table Head we bore off to the northeast bound for Battle Harbour.

Bob Chancey and Fred Clarke had argued all the way from Hooping Harbour to Quirpon, about when the cabbage goes in the pot for jiggs' dinner. Later, they got into a row over whether the salt fish Fred had 'put a-soak' overnight had been watered long enough to have with the brewis for breakfast. Mack, the Skipper, didn't care: growing up on the Straight Shore, he had "eaten enough salt fish to pave Water Street"; he was having sausages instead. The rest of us tucked into the salt fish, the thinner bits being 'light' to 'just right' and the thicker pieces 'salt as the brine.' That suited Fred, who claimed that the thin fish had less flavour than a boiled sock and that, actually, all the fish had been soaked too long. Philip and David garnished theirs with scruncheons. Dad, never a picky eater, dug into it without saying anything and put a dollop of molasses on his brewis; Uncle Chester's preference was for sugar.

We saw thousands of birds on our way up the coast, including large gatherings of shearwaters and some fulmars. Bob speculated there might be areas of turbulence, upwellings carrying shrimp and krill to the surface where one part of the Labrador Current splits off the main stream and flows southwest into the Gulf of St. Lawrence. There were icebergs, growlers and bergy bits everywhere. Fred likes to hear the crackle of the iceberg-ice melting in his otherwise neat Johnny Walker. You realize how heavy ice really is, the immense inertia it has, when you try to lift even the smallest chunk aboard with the dip net.

Mack threaded our way into Battle Harbour by the south entrance, which is, apparently, considered to be very tricky. We tied up near the old Baine Johnston premises where all hands went ashore, with the exception of Uncle Chester and the Skipper who, as always, stayed aboard. Mack did maintenance on the twin, 140-horsepower General Motors diesel engines, and Uncle Chester, who knows people in every cove on this part of the coast, received visitors. It is a place steeped in history, and just the fact of being in that fabled harbour was a thrill for Philip and me. We poked around the old rooms and stages and visited the general store, which, in itself, was to go back in time. On a headstone, nearly hidden in the grass behind the small but remarkable wooden church, the inscription beneath the name read: "Faithful servant of Baine Johnston & Co." That, in a nutshell, sums up the fish merchant history of the entire coast. We had planned to stay there for the night but, anxious to get north, we left and anchored-off at Fishing Ships Harbour, just coming on dark. Speaking of fishing merchants: Fishing Ships Harbour is where Uncle Lewis had, for years, based his very profitable Labrador operations in the salt fish trade. Before we left Fishing Ships Harbour, Uncle Chester pointed out to us where Uncle Lewis' rooms, and the shop he owned, were located and where he lived in the summers and died twenty-one years ago. Fred commented on how the new community stage had replaced most of the small, family-owned rooms and stages, which were beginning to fall into disrepair all around the harbour. He lamented the "insidious socialism" the federal government was foisting on the Newfoundland fisheries, even though, as manager of the Bait Service, he had to be part of it.

There was no more than a draft of wind out of the southwest when we left Fishing Ships Harbour to go north up the coast as far as Black Bear River, about a five-hour run. We intended to 'try' the river, stay the night and then fish our way south over the next four or five days. We had a fine time along: sitting in the cockpit playing crib, sorting out salmon flies, yarning, drinking gallons of coffee – laced with rum for some – as the high, post-solstice sun got 'over the yard arm.' There was only a ripple on the North Atlantic, fecund with whales, birds, and icebergs. We had enough grub aboard to last until Christmas, but had somehow run out of Carnation milk, so we put into Snug Harbour and got a dozen cans at the small, seasonal shop.

The weather can change in minutes on the coast of Labrador. It was 76 degrees sitting at the wharf in Snug Harbour with the wind off the land. But in the half-hour we were there, the wind had backed around to the east, come in off the Labrador Current, and the temperature dropped to 42 degrees. The forecast was for that to freshen and back further into the northeast. Mack said he didn't like the idea of riding at anchor in Black Bear Bay in a northeasterly and Dad agreed. Instead we decided to take the sheltered route through Venison Tickle to Hawke Harbour, and on through Squasho Run to Caplin Bay where, that evening and all the next day, we had the most extraordinary sea trout fishing imaginable.

Extraordinary, but not necessarily the best, if trout fishing is supposed to present a challenge. The trout – thick, silver sea-run brook trout – all from 1½ to 6 pounds, were only too willing to be caught. We were fishing in cold, crystal-clear salt water at a spot where it flowed river-like from one basin into another, changing directions with the tides. You could sometimes see two or three large trout chasing your fly, even after it was lodged in the jaw of another. At first, we used large, red and white bucktail streamers; then I tried the smallest fly I had, a chewed up Black Gnat, and still they came. I tied on flies that were so outlandish they would look gaudy in one of Carman Miranda's hats, and I put a hook through the cork filter from a cigarette butt: no difference, they were addicts. Philip caught a trout that still had in its jaw a fly it snapped off Bob's cast a minute earlier. They were ravenous, yet so firm, fat and strong they obviously weren't starving. Fred, Philip and I got fed up with it, so we moved to a small stream rattling into the bay a hundred yards up the shore, obviously too small, even in spate, to be home to these fish. We hiked up a ways, put on small, conventional dry flies – Quill Gordons, Brown Hackles and Royal Coachman – and had a very satisfactory afternoon fishing for eight- to ten-inch 'muds.'

∾

We had great trout fishing at Pinsent's Arm and two good, memorable days salmon fishing at Shinney's Waters on our way south. We got to Battle Harbour, at 4:45 in the afternoon and stayed there overnight. The forecast was for light to moderate northwesterlies, so we anticipated a fine time along the next day, "The glorious twelfth." We left early, on a direct course for Cape Bauld, which took us close to the austere, aloof Belle Isle, then on to Canada Bay and reached Roddickton before dark. Dad and Fred drove home from Roddickton to return to work. Bob, Philip and I stayed aboard with Mack and Uncle Chester for the trip back to Conception Bay.

Although the fishing was extraordinary, it was not the fishing we talked about after dinner on Christmas Day or when Dad and Fred came down to Salmonier on a stormy weekend in March. We talked about the haunting spectre and history of the rusting, burned out whaling station at Hawke Harbour and yarning with old Ace Wentzell about life on the coast, how hard the good times were; how good the hard. We talked about Snug Harbour and Tub Harbour and when the cabbage should go in the pot. We also talked about the comforts of the oil range in the *Hemmer Jane's* galley when the wind turned to the northeast, and of the warmth and camaraderie in the cockpit and the close-up colours of icebergs when the sun shines with the wind off the land.

There were other things about that trip that stayed with me: the opportunity to learn from Uncle Chester – the youngest of my grandfather Dawe's seven sons – something about that man, who had died eight years before I was born. And the memory, the image, of my father sitting alone in the cockpit, wrapped against the chill in an old, hooded, toggle-fastened navy great coat, smoking yet another cigarette – the rhythm of its glowing seeming to mark the patterns of his thoughts – listening to the Labrador night.

On the Hemmer Jane, c. 1968
L-R: *Jack Pratt, Fred Clarke, Philip Pratt, Bob Chancey, Christopher Pratt*

1971
Boat in Sand

When I was growing up, boats were far more important in rural Newfoundland than cars and trucks. Small boats had always been the backbone of the Newfoundland economy and the ability to handle them the measure of a man. They symbolized our way of life.

I did the print *Boat in Sand* in 1961, at a time when things were changing very rapidly in Newfoundland. It seemed to me that traditional and viable social structures were being systematically discredited.

I was living in Sackville at the time, working in a small, unventilated room, searching for techniques to make the image work. It took me four frustrating months, but it was very satisfying to see the boat emerging from the paper, very pale at first, but stronger with each printing. It seemed to appear out of the fog. I had made a window in the 'studio' wall, and through it I could see St. Mary's Bay.

January 1, 1972

I went off on my skis this clear, blue morning into and beyond Labyrinth Pond. Up on the marshes, a mile from the road – paths covered by the snow and trees not big enough to cut – the land is exactly as it would have been a hundred years ago. I noticed lots of rabbit tracks on the way and this afternoon Philip and I went in and set fourteen snares. I haven't done that for a very long time. I keep thinking I'm against hunting – at least, against killing for sport. One day last winter I took my 16-gauge and went looking for ducks. Hunting seemed to sharpen my awareness of everything – sounds, scents, colours. Perhaps it makes you belong more intimately to the land, not just a visitor. Hunting, you become part of the life-death force.

1972

He went to Topsail with his parents every June, and lived in houses with woodstoves and deep, cool wells and learned to love the taste of scalded cream and sweet, chilled milk; the smell of caplin drying in the fog, spruce boughs, bogs, brooks and waterfalls, trampled grass inside musty canvas tents and hay-making in the fields. He learned to love the sound of birds: fox sparrows and white-throated sparrows, terns at their fishing and snipe winnowing at night above the muffled rhythm of a distant train. And he learned to love the look of sun-warped, wrinkled air rising off the hayloft sill, the blue sky from its dark interior, the look of Ursula and sunlight in small rooms.

1972

I change things as I go because, for me, working with a subject is an act of research into that subject: my feelings change, my understanding grows and what I find has to go into the work and thereby change it. There is continuous feedback and growth in this organic process, so it is useless to try to foresee an end product. That would be to ignore the most vital part of the creative process.

1973

They counted out their years in Christmases. Every year at Christmas the talk would be of "last Christmas," or the last Christmas they had lived at Bristol's Hope, or if this would be "poor so 'n so's" last Christmas. The words *last* and *Christmas* seemed inseparably linked.

I had a "last Christmas" of my own when I was seven. I asked too many questions about why Santa often missed the children down the hill on Flynn Street and Lyons Square and Cofield's Lane – and why he never came to Maxie Silver, who lived right next door.

We had some primitive electric wreaths, just cardboard rings wrapped with chenille. No gluttony of baubles or megawatts of outdoor lights ever stood so defiantly against the winter solstice.

I was in the living room this morning before daylight, when I could see only the brightest ornaments, shining out of the dark corner of the room. Every year I am afraid we carry Christmas to excess – the mystery of gifts – but I know that, over the years, we have given our children good Christmases and I'm not sorry.

The Christmas tree will come down today.

1973

I stopped work at 3:00 and went out for a skate with John and Ned, for about an hour. The exercise and exposure doesn't seem to have made my cold any worse. I have worked since then. I enjoy painting; I like the way formal relationships develop, creating the illusion of light and space and time through subtle changes in tone and colour, in lines and planes.

It is a cold night, snowing very lightly. The rink will need to be cleared again, if the tide doesn't fracture and ruin the ice.

∾

I went skating again today, this time playing hockey with John and Ned from 4:00 to 5:00. I love to skate. Sometimes I dream

I can skate very well, smooth and fast, effortlessly. Sometimes I dream I am gliding, levitated along down a street or a path. Waking, I know that comes from a memory of skating. Sometimes I dream I am swimming in warm, crystal-clear water, floating, gliding through the water like a porpoise.

It's a still winter night. I have done all I can do this day.

1973

Every spring, the pack ice drifts southward from the Arctic to the coasts of Newfoundland. It lies offshore in an immense, shimmering white field. Winds and currents raft it to the land where it threatens, scours and retreats. Every year, when spring is moving northward in the rest of North America, the ice convinces me that we are, our planet is, an accident, a single cell of life adrift in a geophysical infinity.

1973

The Strait of Belle Isle is the only place where you can see the continent of North America from the island of Newfoundland. You get that wonderful offshore feeling, the meeting all around of land with sea. You know that this place has a definition more natural and precise than arbitrary, legislated parallels and longitudes. In the winter, great wild places like the Strait of Belle Isle come into their own.

Ice in the Strait of Belle Isle, looking toward Labrador

1974

The very word "Labrador" was magic to me when I was a child. That was before the Churchill Falls development and the iron mines. The tales I heard were of the coast, of hardship and heroism, of nature on a giant scale: a land where the fish were innumerable, the icebergs immense, the storms unimaginable. Labrador was the parent and Newfoundland the child: a boy who survived its disciplines would thereby be a man. Here in St. Mary's Bay, we live at a latitude south of London, Paris and Victoria, yet we have plants and animals in common with the Arctic tundra. The Labrador Current is a relentless flood of molten ice, the bloodstream of our near sub-arctic climate.

1974

I was in Gambo, or maybe it was Clarenville, one day, before they shut the railway down. I used to go to stations just to look around and absorb their neutrality. They looked foreign in that environment, perhaps because their architecture was ubiquitous and not particular to Newfoundland. Being virtually the same from coast to coast, they imposed a taste of Fredericton Junction or a Prairie whistle stop on rural Newfoundland.

I had not been on a train in Newfoundland since 1954. I often made short trips by train when traveling in other parts of Canada: Montreal to Kingston and Toronto, Toronto to London or Niagara-on-the-Lake. I liked the weedscapes by the railway yards and at level crossings, entering cities or passing through small towns; I liked the split-second glimpses into other peoples' lives. It was like watching Burchfield and Hopper paintings flashing by. There was a Hopper feeling, a compelling ordinariness, about these local stations too. Unlike churches, houses or parish halls, they demanded neither allegiance nor respect.

1975

Before I knew what art was, or what it was supposed to be, I was convinced it was something real and that it could be anything. That occurred to me long before I found out that other people had also decided that anything could be selected, identified, and be designated art. For example, before I knew anything about DADA, I believed that picturesque, photogenic, beautiful or even magnificently ugly things had no more claim to precedent than the unadorned, unlit cupboard door outside my bedroom. The sun, a mighty presence, had no greater reality than the 40-watt bulb whose terrestrial energy it had ordained.

As a child lying in bed in darkness relieved only by the dim, distant and widely separated streetlights of wartime St. John's, nothing scared me more than the awareness of what seemed an enormous absurdity: that things existed at all. It was equally impossible to imagine nothing. It was yin and yang, black and white, but the contemplation of nothing was not as troubling and difficult as the fact that there was something: why, how, from where? This immense sense of absurdity made my stomach churn as a child and still fills and frustrates me. In the face of it, all things are equal in the fact that they exist.

1975

Students at the Glasgow School of Art were urged to spend their summers touring the great galleries of Europe. I spent mine working as a surveyor on an American military base in Newfoundland. We were environmental artists without knowing it: pinpointing coordinates, striking lines as straight as sight, shaving grades to runway specs, laying out spider webs of steel to take the weight of giant storage tanks.

The radar-bellied Super Constellations landed and took off incessantly, patrolling the Atlantic, looking for incoming bombers and "Red" submarines, cranking up the tensions of the Cold War years. There were other tensions too, inherent in peacetime military life, the tensions of life on the base itself. Everything reflected rank: housing, mess halls and clubs were all separate quarantines. There was immense frustration in that microcosm of society. Although the personnel seemed pent-up to explosiveness, there were few incidents. It was all constrained by structures, physical and social: massive concrete buildings with endless corridors of navy grey and prescribed R & R.

Glasgow School of Art, c. 1958

1975

I am back at the Grace, visiting. Mary is asleep; she seems more comfortable. She has been miserable for the past six months, ever since we lost the twins she was carrying. I phoned her parents.

I have not come to loathe this hospital room, like I thought I would. So far, my experience of this hospital has not been such as to produce loathing. In reality, it is very like one of my paintings: crisp, bare walls – no cracks or irregularities where dirt can hide – a clean, efficient meeting of horizontals and verticals and an interesting play of tones from surface to surface. Even the curtain-screen is interesting: a simple textural foil for the completely flat walls, with irregular vertical folds and a transparent section at the top providing contrast. The furniture is functional and unadorned. The radiators, like the ones I imagined in *The Visitor* painting, have colours that are pale grey-greens and yellows. The evening sunlight coming in this room on the seventh floor makes interesting patterns: direct light and shadow, indirect glow and reflection. Sunlight is sunlight, anywhere. This room would actually make a half-decent studio – have I been painting hospitals without knowing it; the residue of some memory or fear I had as a child?

∾

The sun has gone down and the room is now half-lit. Light from the corridor becomes stronger than the light from day. Soon there will be no day; the darkness that will occupy the room will emphasize the brightness of the corridor where the nurses come and go, where there is help. It is the source of light, but it harbours mystery. What do they know that I do not? In the morning, gradually, the light from outside will overcome the corridor's authority. I will come back then. I hope Mary can come home.

CHRISTOPHER PRATT

47

1976

For centuries before the cod stocks collapsed, tens of thousands of Newfoundlanders left home to make a living elsewhere: Boston, Brooklyn, Canada. Communities that harboured, say, two hundred souls in their heyday, would have become substantial towns if more people found it possible to stay. But the resources of this island, at least as they were managed, kept only a privileged few in style. Having to leave the outports wasn't new, but abandoning whole communities was. That started in the 1960s with the Smallwood government's "resettlement" plan, when people from isolated settlements were enticed or forced to move to places where, in some small way, the expectations of Confederation could be met. Seemingly overnight, there were abandoned villages all around the coast. Often towing their houses behind their boats like huge, windowed whales, people just packed up and left, leaving behind their way and means of life. In many places only a few, larger buildings remained, such as churches, schools and shops. They were like well-found ships mysteriously abandoned at sea: sound, seaworthy, but with no sign of crew. They stood as memorials until weather and vandals tore them down.

1976

Nothing on earth is so violent as a storm at sea, yet, when it is over, all that energy and chaos resolves itself into long, rounded swells, as measured as rings circling outward from a pebble dropped into a pool.

The breakwater to the north of Long Pond Gut is of standard government design, ubiquitous from Bronte Harbour to the Labrador. The work of engineers, they are abstractions of the old rock-ballast, pile-and-cribbing wharves that were built locally. They look like they came in a box.

Because the breakwater subject was already a general one, I felt no urgency to alter it. We kept our boat at Long Pond and we passed this breakwater to starboard every time we put to sea.

As a child, my son Ned did a drawing of the structure and its tower. I have it in my studio, a memory of many days spent sailing on Conception Bay. It has become an important part of my associations with the place.

1978

I think from my earliest awareness I have ranked the masters of ships very high on my scale of men. I think that, perhaps if I had not become an artist, I would want to be master of a ship, maybe a destroyer, or a big trawler. When I was a boy, I lived close to a world full of stories of men who went to the Labrador and of boys who at an early age skippered their fathers' schooners to Nain. In the war years, sailors and officers in uniform came to our house, officers of the Canadian and Free Norwegian navy, from Corvettes that worked the north Atlantic from St. John's to Murmansk. There are pictures of me with them wearing a Norwegian captain's hat. Something in my coward soul wished to go in those grey ships into the grey Atlantic in search of enemy submarines. I imagined I would cut them down. The Norwegians had a photograph that horrified my mother, of an allied ship ramming a disabled German submarine, with desperate men leaping from its conning tower.

So, owning a boat now is not just a matter of yachting to me: it represents a wish fulfillment, a wish older than any to be good at art, which is somehow accidental in my life. The size of my boat is excessive to my boating needs, but the cold discomfort of sailing through a fog and finding home, standing off these wet, black shores – that is my Labrador.

But wish fulfillment is just that and the wish continues; its fulfillment little more than artifice. When racing, if we win, I show I am for that event a better skipper than a few, fiscally selected peers. When we sail from Halifax to here, I show I have at least more adventure in me than some of them. That hardly makes me master of the *Hood* or *Prince of Wales* or skipper of a vessel fishing in the trenches off the coast of Labrador. What is there is at best the bounty of imagination, so the boating is my opiate, my Xanidu, my Never Never Land.

1978

I had done a graphite drawing of some cliffs, just north of Little Barasway on the Cape Shore. It was essentially an exploration of the patterning of snow on rock, solid rock falling vertically with scree sliding down. While I was doing this, I was aware of a sense of anxiety, a fear of height, that there was nowhere to hold on, no way of getting up. It was a desolate, inanimate and hostile place. Then I thought of putting in the birds, because they are always there, especially ravens, in all weathers and in all seasons. Ravens are frequently the only living things in that environment – they could be flakes of slate, fragments of the cliff that have taken wing. I knew their symbolism and mythology: black birds of ill omen and bad luck, spirits of the dead. I could see those birds as spirits, the voice and embodiment of the inanimate, but I never thought of them as harbingers of grief. In fact, I found them welcoming.

1979

I am never comfortable using music as an analogy for light. I am intolerant of people who describe a sunrise as a symphony. Yet, I think that there are certain qualities of light that hum, like the juxtaposition of natural and artificial light at that time of day when they are in equilibrium, when neither dominates.

Bonavista Bay, c. 1968

1980

We went into St. Philips to visit my parents today. Dad struggles to use his artificial leg, but he is not strong and can hardly manage, so he is in a wheelchair most of the time. It is very sad to see him so reduced, and confused. He accepts it without complaint.

My work has not gone well since I finished the *Trunk* painting three months ago. I am trying to bail it out by returning to an old ambition to do a large, definitive artist/model painting. I have no one posing for me at the present time so I'm working from an old drawing of Bride. This is nothing of a compromise. There is an attitude about the figure that is germane to the idea that the model is more than an object and the artist less than objective – that reality is one thing, and art something else.

But there are issues of light and texture that the drawing does not explain, so I have asked Brenda – whose usual role is to get me out of otherwise irreversible commitments and run interference on awkward phone calls – to stand in for Bride.

1980

I know some rivers very well; I have walked and fished the length of them, every steady, rattle and bend, from the headwaters to the estuary. Others, I have known only from the pools I've fished, or at a crossing place. That is the difference between being a traveler and a transient. It reminds me of the feeling I used to get when, as a youth, I was a guest at a cousin's summer cabin for a week. I was just an incident in what they would later call 'our summer.' I felt that I could not really be part of it, that the tensions and relationships had a history I didn't share and a future that I wouldn't know. My own past and future seemed to be behind me and in front of me, theirs to the left and right. There were both frontal and lateral infinities.

In Newfoundland, the railway often ran close by the sea and in many places, the tracks were laid along the beach. You crossed them to go walking on the shore. I always like those parallels: crisp, iron-brown rails against sea greys and blues and greens, regular but ragged lines of waves, back to the sky. It seemed to be a perfect metaphor.

Jack Pratt fishing at MacCallums on the Southeast River, 1958

1982

I am back in Salmonier, alone. This afternoon I drove to Placentia and down the Cape Shore as far as Great Barasway. There was a lot of snow and the bush on the side of the road had grown in. Sometimes it was like driving along a park trail. I stopped on the Southeast River, where our cabin used to be. It burned down over twenty years ago and the only things remaining are the square concrete posts it stood on and the ruins of the fireplace. Trees are growing where the living room used to be. I don't know why, but I said a silent prayer in memory of my father. I can't say I don't believe but I don't think I do, so it was like talking to myself, talking from and to the consciousness of which I am the privileged, temporary custodian. There were many things just out of reach, just out of focus. How sad it is to articulate the questions but be incapable of finding the answers. That is where I am trapped – perhaps everybody is.

They have bullied a new road down the Cape Shore. It is still a wound, but that will heal. Seeing the houses at Great Barrisway reminded me of how much of my work began there: *Clothesline, House and Barn*, and indirectly, *Young Woman with a Slip*. I had a very romantic attitude about life on that shore, an attitude probably seldom shared by those who had endured its frequent hardships. But romance is neither a product of nor an antidote for hardship. There seems to be little of what I took to be determination left. Perhaps circumstance has drained it away. It no longer speaks to me as clearly as it used to. Still, I could use a new "Cape Shore."

1982

There is a lot of snow and the wind is blowing very hard. It is the kind of night when wind, waves and temperature combine, making ice, and glass-sharp crystals blow inland, cutting shapes that hikers find in summer and take home for the mantelpiece, because they 'look like ducks.' Such is the creative process: a storm under the cover of darkness, shaping things in turmoil and privacy – leaving souvenirs.

1983

We went to Oshawa for the opening of Mary's Retrospective at the Robert MacLaughlin Gallery. Her work holds up exceptionally well. It is technically and physically substantial, concise, condensed and contained. It is intellectually honest: apparent without being superficial, literate without being narrative, and articulate without being glib. Any reference to her use of slides tends to become negative if you don't approve of photo-realism, defensive if you do. Historically, her method needs no defense, as the use of photographic and pre-photographic devices is as old as the visual arts themselves. Her personal use of photographs is entirely contemporary and her paintings are incalculable enrichments of the slides from which they proceed. They are an enrichment that is both visual and spiritual and proceeds from her deep understanding of the subjects she chooses to paint, with a love and mastery of the painting process, unique on the contemporary Canadian art scene. In her work, the 35mm slide is brought together with the techniques of Chardin; a Renaissance concern with what looks real, brought together with a highly literate, post-Freudian awareness of what is real. Hers is a truly original departure; its uniqueness is so subtle it can easily be overlooked.

1983

I think the representational component of my work created an expectation of narrative detail, even romantic content, as in, say, Andrew Wyeth's or Ken Danby's realism. The more so because I lived in a place that was thought to be picturesque, folksy and quaint. People looked for narrative where they would never have expected it in the abstraction, the mainstream minimalism, of Yves Gaucher or Charlie Gagnon's prints or, on a grander stage, Joseph Albers or Piet Mondrian. In its absence they saw my work as being cold, lifeless, somehow sterile, and concluded I must have ice water in my veins. They missed the point.

That may have been my fault, of course. I thought to depart from representational content but I didn't, because I believed the errand of the eye is to recognize, and it insists on finding things and imagines them where they are not. I no longer believe this is universally true. Most people will try to spot a cow or a car or an elephant or a landscape in abstractions – they do the Rorschach thing. However, others do see a painting for what it is – a painting and not necessarily a painting of something. Yet, even for essentially non-objective painters, the use of visual clues or distractions remained, such as signs or puzzles with words, collage and other techniques and inferences. These became almost universal, a hook whereby you are encouraged to believe the work is about something.

The subject matter is important to me. I am not immersed in the world or philosophies of art; I am not concerned with movements, isms or manifestos, or their small and big 'p' politics. My art, if it is art, is not about art; it may not seem to be about life either, but it originates there. I am preoccupied with the fact of existence. I depend on the redemption of light. Light is life.

1984

I am concerned with surfaces, not their superficial textures and narrative details, but the way light plays on them and defines their essential shapes. Perhaps I should say 'subsurfaces' because I think a lot of things that we think of as 'deep' are actually very near the surface and accessible, just underneath the first coat of paint, the cosmetics of vanity and circumstances alike. The sciences dig deep, looking for first causes, but often there is too much science and not enough sense, too much investigation that challenges and questions instinct.

There is little excuse for realism in art. It is not enough that the objects or situations portrayed in a work are significant. The work should be the embodiment of that significance and not just a representation of it.

Art is frustration arousing in its maker: emotions without an object, love with no one to embrace, hatred with no one to strike, and fear with nothing to flee. Perhaps love, fear and hate are the same thing physiologically and different from each other only in respect of circumstance.

1984

Critics say that I remove all trace of humanity from my work, that it is devoid of all human warmth and feeling, especially my architectural things. What do they want and what do they mean by human? Humans measure and build with levels, rulers and squares, transits and theodolites. We proclaim a *right* angle. It is the weather, the wind and the rain and the sun that cause paint to peel, boards to crack and fall, roofs to sag, chimneys to crumble. Yet, people see the evidence of that activity as humanizing. When I ignore those things and focus on what is deliberate and structural, then I re-humanize. The patina of time and moss softens the confrontation with what we do and who we are – instant content that is as superficial as the moss itself. We pride ourselves in ploughing straight furrows in the land, steering a great circle course across the sea and predicting trajectories across the sky. Then why is it humanizing to depict the way the sun peels paint and cracks wood and the rain stains clapboard with nail-head rust?

However, I do love light; it is warm yet geophysical; it is the non-organic sustainer of organic life, the real and the abstract. When I draw, it caresses where I cannot touch.

Winter / Spring, 1984

Every time I do a silkscreen print I swear it will be my last. But despite the labour and health risks of doing it all by hand in what has become a cottage industry environment, I am still attracted to the aesthetics of the medium: the flat, unapologetic, almost textureless surface and crisp linearity, combined with the acceptable and instructive constraints – disciplines – of the fabric itself. Watching the image develop as successive stencils get made and printed one over another is like watching something emerge out of a fog.

I have now punched in four days – two of them fourteen-hour marathons – trying to get the sky gradation for the *Yacht Wintering* print to go right. I have had to over-print all 120 boards three times. Some of the flaws may get covered up as I print the darker parts of the boat itself. What with having to pull the paint on scrap papers at least six times to get the blend to knit, I never had enough paint left on the screen to print more that four or five copies – after which I had to clean up and start again.

I figure I pulled the squeegee a minimum of 800 times to come up with the seventy or so copies that will make it to the next stage. As always, I will use the losers for stencil, registration and colour trials. The print shop reeks of paint, mineral spirits, lacquer and acetone, so I'm glad to be out of there for the weekend. I have brought the screen itself back to the studio to work on the next stencil between now and Monday.

I was so tired that I had a mind to call Denise after supper and tell her not to come up, but figure drawing is so different from screen printing, the contrast so total, that it accesses a different source of energy. I print in a cold, bright fluorescent room with the windows open wide to the outside world and fans whining arrhythmically in an effort to exchange the air. I draw from life incandescently, in a warm, private space where there is music, or silence interrupted only by occasional, interesting chat that does not disarm but often mitigates that intuitive, intense and mutually productive tension, the heightened awareness and intimacy that is at the heart of the creative process. It is the subject – not the medium – that ordains the aesthetic. I try to save some of that to energize the hours of my more abstract, less spontaneous work.

1984

We drew from life every day at the Glasgow School of Art: we were taught to blend light into dark and to use cast shadows and reflected light to render three dimensions on a two-dimensional plane. We were told to think of line as an expression of volume, not just shape, and to move around the figure to find a sequence of contour lines, imagining how section-lines would look at the calf, thigh or waist. We made sculptures in clay, learned to consider tactile properties, and were told always to remember symmetry.

When I quit my job at Memorial and moved here in 1963, I hadn't drawn from life in four years, not since I left Glasgow and returned to study at Mt. Allison in 1959. That had diminished me as an artist. I have always believed that the ability to draw, the process of getting from zero to one, is essential, and my instinct was to leapfrog those years and begin again where I left off in Scotland.

I had a romantic notion of what a studio should be, reflecting the stereotypes of artists in smocks wearing black berets, like something out of *La Bohème*. That studio had high ceilings with large, loosely curtained windows overhead and imposing oak easels holding huge waiting canvasses. There were platforms and divans piled with pillows, where models would recline on patterned, oriental fabrics that receded into the gloom. In my imagination, it was out of Ingres through Manet, Matisse and Modigliani, with echoes of such lesser lights as Jules Pasçin.

My bare white room on the edge of the Avalon wilderness would be a far cry from those imagined studios, but with the unexpected gift, over time, of being able to find models virtually next door. Although they knew nothing of art and artists, I think most of them could have handled that Parisian studio. Anything would have been better than standing on that cold, uninsulated floor or sitting for hours on a hard wooden box, but it was all as much an adventure for them as it was for me.

My ideas about drawing from the nude must have been pre-programmed too. I couldn't see my studio as a context for my work and made little reference to it when I drew: I left out evidence of furnishings, works-in-progress standing against my studio walls, the models' clothing thrown or folded on a chair, and ignored the artificial light. I imagined the models located in their own bedrooms and arranged lights and provided them with props to prove the point.

There were the benefits of continuity and evolution as well. My work always related to individuals and I often used the name of the model in my titles. Bernadette posed for me, off and on, for three years. Later, I was able to do sequential drawings and paintings of Brenda, Denise and Dianne. Donna posed for me continuously at first and then periodically for fourteen years. At one point, influenced by books of the work of Alfred Stieglitz and Edward Weston, and by my friend John Reeves, I set up a small, amateur darkroom in my studio and did a series of photographs of Donna. I have kept some of the black and white prints, but I have never exhibited them. With Donna's permission, I gave the slides – Kodachrome transparencies – to Mary. It was a privilege and luxury to work with girls who had no preconceptions about life in the studio. The precedents they brought were from their world, not mine.

1984

I don't know how I would have fared with professional models. Maybe they would have compromised my privacy through inadvertent references to other artists' studios. Perhaps they would have done standard art school poses, kept an eye on the clock and been very nonchalant about the process. I think it's better to have models who find some excitement in the studio, a sense of adventure and participation, of doing something unexpected, just off-center. Sometimes the responsibility I feel for their comfort level gets in the way, but there is a productive tension that otherwise might not be there.

1984

As children, we made tents with blankets draped across some chairs, or propped behind the sofa for a house. Even as a child, I experienced the eroticism of that privacy. That was very long ago. I associated her with that. When I saw her in her coffin, I remembered it.

1984

In this age of enlightened cynicism, who can be anthropo-morphic about the wind, the seasons, the moon, the stars or the night itself? I have never seen a ghost or felt a presence where a presence ought to be. Spirits are within us, not abroad. Burchfield was a romantic, he wanted to be known as a romantic realist, and anthropomorphism was central to his romanticism. It may be to all romanticism. That is what I edit from my reaction to things: the tree branch that looks like a hand or claw, the clouds that look like elephants, a sky that is menacing and everything else. In a way, all art is romantic. It is already romantic to believe that things can have a presence, a spirit that exceeds their surfaces, that two plus two can equal five. "There is something there." What *is* there? Sunlight on a wall?

1984

The work that came back from Mira's included some of the most basic, austere pieces I have ever made: the collage *Atlantic*, which is simply two pieces of grey card butted together to make a square along a horizontal line dividing sea from sky, and the collage studies for *Ocean Racer*. The concept of ocean racing immediately suggests action, wind and wave, froth and foam, "all their gear, tackle and trim," with the boat never at rest. No objects could be more devoid of the illusion of movement than these collages. They are designs, intellectual exercises, based on sail and rigging patterns that have nothing to do with the guts of ocean racing. How did I get so far from the meat and sinew of things? I have retreated from that hard edge of abstraction, but not far enough. What has killed the poetry and left me arranging lines and tones: is there nothing underneath the surface of the pond, behind the wall, through the window, in the room, or on the mind of the model? On the other hand, is that poetry too, even if it is all just a matter of surfaces, of planes reflecting light? Can there be mystery in anything seen in such sharp focus, so clearly seen as the images I make, or does mystery need blurred lines? Does delineation imply there is no mystery – ignorance perhaps – but no unknown?

I'm not sure that I really know why a certain subject interests me. I think I do, and that it is often romantic or sentimental, intellectually contrived or morbid. I find out what the issue really is as the thing develops. The issue becomes the painting itself: what it is telling me, where it is taking me emotionally, where it is leading me aesthetically, in terms of formal, structural priorities, mood, understanding. It is like a layered analysis.

1984

It is a cool, grey day after the most prolonged period of truly warm weather that I can remember in Newfoundland. We motored from Holyrood to Long Pond, having decided not to race the second day of the Newfoundland and Labrador Keel Boat Championships. We have had some very beautiful sailing in the warm evenings, but the racing has been unpleasant, leaving no time to go cruising.

When the wind is fresh and the weather good and *Dry Fly* slips through the sea with all the ease and authority she has, I feel better than at any other time. With the water rolling past the leeward rail, it is as if the boat becomes an extension of my being.

I have seen the day go round at sea, and felt the press of darkness on my eyes. But sailing has been love and hate: loving the feel of the boat, its looks and lines and those euphoric evenings, hating the frustrations and responsibility and always the expense. Boating has brought out the best and worst in me.

1984

When I was a boy reading *Tom Sawyer*, *The Hardy Boys*, and my father's favourite, *Horatio Alger*, I always had a strong inclination, when something exciting was happening, to put the book down and go do it myself. Even if it was February, the description of a baseball game was enough to get me on the phone to arrange with a friend to go, then and there, for a 'catch.' The description of hunting or other outdoor adventures would trigger a similar response irrespective of the season. I would wind up climbing all five hundred feet of the Southside Hills, imagining I was conquering Everest, or go on safaris with my Daisy 'Red Ryder' BB rifle in search of 'homeless cats.' I'm not pretending to be a man of action, as opposed to letters – I am neither – but I have always tried to make dreams into reality. I can't be bothered to 'dream the (demonstrably) impossible dream.'

Proud Mary, 1974
Back: Barby, Garry McManus, Christopher, Ned, Bob Halliday,
Marie Christine DeMessines; Front: Mary, Anne

1985
Fredericton

Even though she knew it was likely for the last time, Mary said goodbye to her father as if she were going uptown or around to Mrs. Bailey's to shop. With the same control and human dignity, he also said goodbye as if he would shortly be going to the office for the day. Yet, there was some quality of voice and circumstance, some level of communication more direct than speech. She told me that on the previous night, he had sung to her "When I Grow Too Old to Dream." He had sung that to her as an infant, the first time he held her in his arms. Was that a sense of theatre, or is all theatre a mirror of such small realities? Before we left Fredericton, after all the encounters and learning of his 93 years, he said religion "was still and could only be as the faith of a child."

The West home on Waterloo Row in Fredericton
Still in the family, it is now a heritage building

1985

We left Salmonier in the dark morning and drove to the airport through falling snow. The day came on us as if white paint were mixing into black, one drop at a time. The plane took the dirt road down to Halifax – a very rough flight. I hate flying anyway. The drive from Halifax to Fredericton was slow, the road slippery in places. Mary has not been emotional but she will need to be. She wants to go to the funeral home alone.

April 4, 1985
Holy Thursday

It is just above freezing on a bright spring morning. I can see the otter on the ice edge at the running in, drops of water jewel-like on his coat, black and shining in the morning sun. He must be living well on spent fish, trout and salmon, returning to the sea.

I never bring my lips or eyes into contact with the water there, never scoop up a cupful in my hands to spill across my wrists and run out through my fingers. I drink from the spring of life as if through a straw. I have quenched my thirst safely, cautiously, never risking falling in or even getting wet.

It is a still, moonlit night. White ice floats down the smooth black river. I sense the dark mystery of the wilderness behind Philip's hill. An April night: it could be Christmas Eve.

Salmonier Pond in spring

1985

Should I continue following my nature down dark corridors? Is that my nature, or do those images seem more sophisticated, technically easier? When I close my eyes and daydream, when I'm half-awake or half-asleep and images appear unfettered by a more pragmatic consciousness, they are usually images of dark corridors, visits to strange rooms. As I walk around, I am arrested by the totally non-picturesque: an open cupboard, a sordid stairway, an ice machine. I notice these things as I pass. I have to go in search of images that come from experience. I have to reconstruct my references to LeMarchant Road or Topsail, Bay Roberts or Ocean Pond, but dark corridors just flash across my mind and interrupt my ordinary sight.

1985

It is a beautiful spring morning, bright, clear sunshine and fairly mild. I removed the tape from around the bedroom window and as I opened it, for the first time since November, I heard, as if on cue, the honk of geese circling above the open water. It gave me shivers up and down my spine to see them settle in the pond, breaking the smooth black surface into silver beads as they came in. That, and finding bulbs sprouting in the flowerbeds when I threw off the boughs and snow, made me realize again how powerful the evidence of renewal and rebirth is at this time of year. It's Easter Monday after all, the continuity of life, if not of individuals. It clouded over as the day went by: the geese stayed, the otter fished (I saw it with an eel), trout breached in the newly open 'running out,' on their way back to the sea.

1985

We drove to Grates Cove via Old Perlican yesterday. I hadn't been past Carbonear for over twenty years. The new road no longer dips and twists through all the villages, but some old sections are still in use so we took them coming back. Great-grandfather Pratt was a preacher on that shore in the 1880s: Uncle Ned was born at Western Bay and Uncle Cal at Blackhead. The land is high and the cliffs very steep and frightening, especially near Flambro Head. There are some once substantial houses, evidence of earlier prosperity, often set in groves of aspen trees. This afternoon I printed the tree-shadow stencil for *Spring at My Place*, which I am working on, over a copy of an abandoned print: the resulting hybrid reminds me of Ochre Pit Cove.

1985

Another beautiful day if calm and clear is beautiful. There is a touch of frost on the grass and mist rising off the black water. Foam bubbles from the river shine silver on the surface of the pond, back-lit by the sunlight. I hear a grey jay somewhere. What harm if we construct our own reality out of these surface things? What harm if we imagine an eternity that includes ourselves? Whatever the cosmos is up to, the evolution of the human spirit with its sense of beauty and order, must be its finest hour.

1985

After I printed, I took the long drive through St. Vincent's and Trepassey, up the Southern Shore. It was an extraordinary, dramatic day: very windy, sunlight alternating with shadow and whiteouts, the absolute of winter on the Southern Avalon. The sea was unbelievably green. There were fields of ice and slush along the shore, like ripples moving through ice cream, that softened the sharp edges of the waves. Yet, they looked sinister and threatening.

Anchored in the bight between Great Colinet Island and Point La Haye, an oil rig and its tender, a monster and its guardian dog, looked like creatures from another world. The hills facing the sea were stripped of snow, patterned only in the furrows and hollows. The wind and light were one, single-shaping, bleaching force from seaward. The Peter's River barrens were an immense flat field of white, the subtle colours beautiful: soft, cool blues, greys and browns, light-struck ridges, shapes of light and drifting snow.

I was reminded, yet again, how far the outports are from St. John's: how far it is from a small wind-penetrated house on Point La Haye to Rennie's Mill Road, from the small kitchens and the local shops, to the restaurants and shopping centres of St. John's. It really is a leap of half a century.

1985

When you arrive at an image intuitively, you don't necessarily know exactly what it means. It emerges from your subconscious like a dream and like a dream it may require analysis and yet never fully yield.

1985

The first race went twice around Little Bell Island and home with a good fresh breeze and sunny periods by noon. *Dry Fly*'s weather. Started with full main and #2 and rode the tri-radial down second leg, then back to #2 upwind. Had a fresher breeze slightly forward of the beam on the fourth leg: reacher and full main. We changed to the Kevlar 3 and a double reef upwind to home. We won! In the afternoon, we went sailing with the double reef and the #4. It was blowing hard, 25-35+. We went to Bareneed on a close reach and came back on a broader reach, the boat averaging about 8 knots in the ever-freshening breeze. It was an exhilarating sail with whitecaps everywhere, showing green through the clean, translucent water. The big little boat moved beautifully across seas that gave her motion but posed no threat. The sky was blue with blue land distant and indigo blue water: all that swish and foam and endless blue, and the clean frigid water slapping us in the face, which is what it's all about.

1985

Driving in to town, I noticed men setting posts in the barrens, presumably for snow fences. I like the straight lines of uniformly spaced verticals all the same height. The contrast of measure, the order against the chaos of post-glacial rubble is very satisfying, reassuring in a way that has nothing to do with a fear of snow blowing across the road. It is a way of controlling the environment mystically as well as physically. I can see how long, straight lines of posts, carefully angled to one another, could define the landscape they were in and take on a Stonehenge-like mystery and presence.

1986

We were at Joyce Zeman's last night to celebrate the opening of my retrospective at the AGO, which she curated. Ron Bloore, Dorothy Cameron, Claude Breeze, Tony Urquhart, Bruce Parsons, and many others were there. It was heartwarming, as so many facets of this experience have been. Ron and the 'Big D' rarely go anywhere, but they had been at the opening. I was very moved by the fact that they got out for me. I feel like I still know those artists we met in 1969, when I did the Canada Council tour from St. John's to Vancouver with David Silcox. Claude Breeze remembered the same things from our first encounter that I did: the party at the Chinese restaurant in Vancouver and some of the good lines, indicating that those times were high points for all of us. It was the same when I saw Ulysee Comtois at the opening of his show at Mira's yesterday. We are becoming part of a generation with memories; witnessing small and simple truths grow into large, exotic legends. It is important to know that all we really do is plant the seeds and that what grows out of them depends on the fertility and receptiveness of the land on which they spread.

May 1986

I spent the morning in St. John's at the Arts and Culture Centre, alone in the galleries with my work. I made notes as if I were a critic, as I had done after the opening of the retrospective at the Vancouver Art Gallery. I felt strangely distant from the paintings in Vancouver; it was like two people with a shared history circling, wondering what their relationship should now be. There was none of that here. It was more like a reunion.

Nonetheless, I came to many of the same conclusions: scale is very important, more so than I had imagined working in a small studio, and not only in a large space. A lot of the print subjects would have benefited from being much larger – maybe three or four times as big, and from the richness and extended chroma of oil paints – *Sunday Afternoon, Night Trestle, Memorial Window, Light Northeast* ... and there are drawings – *Lighthouse Door, The Empty Room* – that could have been paintings as well. So I am thinking 'why not now' and of building a new and larger studio, and in that process finally getting my workspace out of the house.

And perhaps I will. I want to move on to new subjects, and I will scale them up as appropriate. Jeanette has shown so much aptitude for process over the year and a half she has been working in the studio – first as a self-described 'Girl Friday' – that I may set up enlarged versions of some prints and see how she will make out underpainting them, using the prints and my input for direction.

Jeanette Meehan, 1987

1986

Restless after getting back from town and from the doctor, I went out to have another look at the tailrace of the Seal Cove and Topsail hydro station powerhouses. Neither was as I had remembered it; they never are. My ideas can't be found. My places don't exist. What did exist was the strange feeling I always get from seeing water exit from a building with that force and volume. There is a sense of awe and even fear about it – not seeing it flow in as through a culvert, then sucked into the penstocks and escaping, furious, bursting out into the light like a wild stallion escaping capture. I could find that, but not the image; nothing I could photograph would do much more than remind me how I felt.

May 24, 1986

Once, on a 24th of May, behind our house in St. John's, I caught a dozen trout from the Waterford River: a slow, septic section of the river, from just above Symes Bridge to Caribou Hill, with gelatinous water wavering through crawling stones. The riverbanks, fecund with weeds and water plants: lush, septic-fertilized, unnatural accidents, seeding from the English gardens of the rich upstream. The river full of fat, slime-yellow trout, ragged-lipped, torn-finned, slack-vented German Browns. I was very happy.

Once, on a 24th of May, I felt the sun immaculate at Big Barachois, breaking hot through icy veils of fog. The sand, weedless, hard and clean, with broken China shells and on the hummocks spare, hard grass. In the crystal water, tide-rise from the sea, firm, heavy, silver trout: living ice, returning to the river from St. Mary's Bay, salt-smelling wind, sun and silver mist, a boat riding on the swell. Burned so deep the bones hummed inside with happiness.

1986

I have looked at land everywhere from Cuslett and Pt. Verde through Bay Roberts and on to Ochre Pit Cove. I would like to be by the sea, but the personal and emotional implications of those daydreams are prohibitive. So I've compromised and settled for more space in my present studio.

I've got 'young' Tom building the extension, but I'm impatient to have the construction over; I want the confusion ended, the clutter cleared. I want to take my shirt and shoes off and feel the world where it is hot and cold, hard and soft. This has been an extraordinary summer and an amazing year, a year of adrenaline, a temporary reprieve from growing old.

Because the show has gone well, there have been moments when I looked life in the face and found it very unbelievably sweet and beautiful. I have seen it smiling back at me, restoring me and healing me, and I believe that I have never been so happy or known such warmth and lightness of being. Is it dangerous to embrace life because it cannot last? And because it is a fickle lover, is it dangerous to open your shirt so that it may wrap you bare in its seductive arms and risk losing it when you love it the most? Is it best to shelter from life's warmth, learn to hate it for its deceit, so you will not mind losing it? There is an intensity of feeling wherein happiness is almost indistinguishable from grief.

So, if this is the Indian summer of what I wished were youth, should I wish it away so that winter will not be so sudden or the frost so cold?

'Young' Tom sharpening his saw

1986

I have admitted before that the tidiness and control in my work is the result of not wanting to be caught goofing-off, not giving it 'the old college try.' When I became a painter, I was determined not to let anyone say that I was living the life of a ne'er-do-well, a bohemian, a lush. When I quit university and later my job at the Extension Service, and decided not to go into my father's business, I was adamant that no one would accuse me of being too lazy to be responsible. Anyone who looked was going to see young Christopher being serious, pursuing art as a grave and noble purpose, not an easy, carefree life.

Is a tidy life more interesting, more commendable, than a cluttered life? Is a monastic life more meaningful than one soiled with human contact? As a child, I sometimes played in attics, which is like playing around in someone's head, having access to another life or at least its traces and its evidence. There seemed to be more chance of finding something interesting, something secret and exciting, in clutter and confusion than in neatness. An attic filled with piles and piles of junk was much more inviting than one with everything boxed on shelves. (As I write, an image of an attic crosses my mind, empty except for some file boxes side by side, not filling all the space available on the bare-board shelves.) The attic with piles of clothes and spilling trunks is emotional, the rows of boxes intellectual. You might find anything in clutter: letters, photographs, toys, underwear. The file boxes would be full of records, accounts and tidied, sanitized histories. I cannot decide between these two, but in my work and in the image that has just flashed through my mind, I choose the second – why?

On the Burin Peninsula

1986
Voyage

Bronte Harbour to Long Pond,
from 1974 and 1977 etc. logs and entries

On June 12, we left Bronte Harbour on Lake Ontario to sail a new 39-foot fiberglass sloop down the St. Lawrence River, across the Gulf of St. Lawrence and home to Newfoundland. There were seven of us, all Newfoundlanders of many generations, born and bred. We couldn't actually sail in the St. Lawrence Seaway. A boat under sail would be a nuisance to commercial shipping in that frequently narrow channel. We didn't hoist sail until we were through the locks and the turbulent Richileau Rapids and well downriver from Québec City. The engine needed to be broken in anyway, and the electrical and other systems wanted checking out.

Except for keeping a constant watch for freighters and respecting their right of way, especially at night, and being very careful in the lock approaches, the lake and river part of the voyage was little more than a very pleasant inland holiday. Having done this before, we knew where we had to be particularly vigilant: tying up and fending off in the locks, watching out for shallows in the basins and anchorage provided for yachts, and again especially at night, noting every buoy we passed in the crooked passage through the Richileau. From the low eye-level of a sailboat's cockpit, almost like standing on the water itself, it was very easy to confuse the navigation aids with the multitude of flashing lights on shore.

Coupled with the little bit of local history we knew, the resonance inherent in the names of the locks was not without its own poetry: Iroquois, Eisenhower, Snell, Beauharnois, St. Lambert ... Half of us had gone to school in Newfoundland before Confederation and learned as much about Africa and India as we did about what was to become our new Canadian heritage. But we didn't pass the Plains of Abraham without notice – General Wolfe and all that was part of British colonial history. To have a better look around, we tied up and spent a night at the Yacht

Club de Québec. That was it, except when all hands came on deck at night to see the bridges and the lights of the old town. Sailing down the river several times has taught me a little geography. I know little more Canadian history now than I knew then.

We hoisted sail just downriver, east-northeast of Isle aux Coudres where, as I remarked to my shipmates, the great Québecois painter Jean Paul Lemieux then lived and worked. We had a fine romp from there to Rimouski on the Gaspé Coast riding a fresh, gusty southwesterly under full sail: a warm wind rich with the scents of spring fields and forests mingled with those of the sea. We ran into a rough choppy seaway in the Gaspé Passage, with a strong tide running against the wind and arguing with the river current. After a night of getting cold and soaking wet, and mindful that this was the first test of the boat's mast and rigging, we put into Riviere au Renard to dry out and make sure we were shipshape before sailing out into the Gulf.

Of course, there were many minor incidents along the way, some mechanical, some personal, some humorous, others more serious. But there was no rancour or discourse, nothing of a confrontational nature to report, as we alternated chores and watches. As for the laughs – the comic's apology that you 'had to be there' must have been coined to cover humour on small boats!

We cast off at dawn the next morning to cross the Gulf of St. Lawrence. We had no sooner cleared the breakwater than we encountered the same rough, wind-against-the-tide lop that we had struggled through from Matane to Riviere au Renard two nights earlier. We had checked out everything and determined that the boat was in great shape. The folks at the fish plant where we had tied up to take on fuel and water gave us a fair sized tub of fresh shrimp. The crew had decided to use them while they were still "good 'n fresh," which meant for breakfast with pancakes. Uncomfortable in the strange company of pancakes, the shrimp resisted digestion and, much the worse for having been eaten, heaved up overboard, back into the waters they came from.

Everything leveled out after the tide turned and we cleared the tip of the Gaspé Peninsula. There was 'weather' in the forecast, but no strong or sustained winds, nothing serious. It was all smooth, exhilarating sailing with southwesterlies continuing fresh on our starboard quarter. When we got north of and abeam to starboard of the Magdalenes, things changed. We were becalmed for three hours with increasingly ominous swells coming at us from the south, and coming on dark, we were met with heavy rain squalls born on a strong breeze out of the southeast, gusting to 35 knots. All that night, we had to beat our way into ragged seas steep-to under a double-reefed main and a small rag of a storm jib. We had five hours worth of it, all the while wondering if we should heave-to or turn 180 degrees and run up through the Gulf under bare poles. I was exhausted; Bob volunteered to stand my watch, but the wind moderated at daybreak and veered around to the northwest, which brought us abeam of Cape North on the northern-most tip of Cape Breton Island in a hurry.

We made good time after that. Crossing the Cabot Strait on a sailor's sleigh ride, careening along on a broad reach with rooster tails of froth and foam leaping from under our transom, we surfed down the slopes of the bigger waves. It was all under a clear blue, high-pressure sky with the sun hot at its solstice zenith and the wind 'cold as Greenland.' It became a sweet and sour afternoon, of sea and salt, sun and celebration. Ahead of us, we could see the loom of the snow-capped Anguille Mountains on the southwest corner of Newfoundland. We whooped and hollered like cowboys every time the speedometer hit a new high. Sam, who happened to have a cowboy hat, put it on. After a minute or two, as all hands predicted, it blew overboard and got swallowed in our wake. We would have gone back for Sam, but there was no going back for his hat. It being the longest day of the year and a fine night in the offing, we decided that there would be no putting into Port aux Basque either. Instead, we would round Cape Ray and roll on to Ramea.

Getting into the harbour at Ramea, the namesake town of that small archipelago, was a small adventure in itself. There are a number of islands in that group as there are many islands comprising Newfoundland. Dismissing the massive granite umbilical that is the Isthmus of Avalon and the feather of sand and shale that connects Port au Port to the local mainland – without which both would be islands – taken together with Ramea and Brunette, Merasheen, Flat Island, Bell Island, Random, Fogo, Change and Exploits and New World Islands, the Grey Islands and the distant Funks, Quirpon and the Sacred Islands and Woods Island and a thousand more, Newfoundland is an archipelago.

It was dark by the time we got to Ramea, and a pea soup, South Coast fog had rolled in out of a clear, indigo blue night. We had the foghorn and the Ramea radio beacon to guide us, but the fog was so thick we couldn't see even a loom of the light until we were almost under it. We had no radar. We could only hope we wouldn't be cluttered or transparent on the radar screen of a trawler somewhere behind us, returning to port with a load of fish. GPS was unheard of and Loran-C was still in its infancy, and we didn't have one anyway. So we crept along under power, watching the log, compass, and depth sounder and taking constant bearings on the Ramea radio beacon with cross-bearings on Cape Race, which was too distant for accurate, close-in navigation. We had one man on the wheel, one using the RDF hand-bearing compass and four on watch – forward, aft, port and starboard. We could hear surf in the rocks and what sounded like a diesel generator in the distance. Then suddenly there was the light, right where it should be, and for that minute with no fog around it at all. A pickup showed up on the wharf and two guys got out and caught our lines. We asked them if it was all right to tie up there and were told, "You'll be ok there, boys, no worry." They asked where we were from and were surprised to hear we were Newfoundlanders. Most sailboats that came there were from Nova Scotia or the States. We heated up a drop of soup, then I, at least, said some words to the close and fishy-smelling darkness, and then I slept.

It was evident the next morning that the fog had settled in. In retrospect, that was fortuitous as it gave us reason to stay there for the day, even though a fisherman told us, "If you wait for the fog to lift, you might be here 'til August month." We bought two big, fresh, firm cod from that fisherman. I say 'bought,' but he wouldn't hear tell of taking money. In the end, he allowed us to buy the fish from his grandson. I gave him ten dollars. I worried afterwards that not accepting the gift and paying more than the going rate might have been taken as condescension, but the youngster had no problem with that. So we roamed around the islands and borrowed a dory to row over to Great Island on the northeast side of the channel that is Ramea Harbour, with the sun high and hot, burning through the fog. Believing that really good, natural food is ruined by fancy cooking, we cooked the cod simply – poached with a few onions, salt, pepper and a shard of salt pork. Then we played cards into the night, and cast off at daybreak the next morning, en route to Grand Bank.

The wind had come in from the northeast, usually a fairly steady flow in Conception Bay, but gusty enough along the South Coast. One minute it seemed to be spanking down off the hills in williwaws and the next minute funneling out through the fjords. But it had blown away the fog and we sailed close-hauled and close-in so we could see that majestic part of the South Coast. When we came abeam of the bleak, grey grandeur of Cape la Hune, we bore off on a close reach for the southwest tip of Brunette Island, which was only a couple of degrees north of our course for Grand Bank.

We had planned to put into Grand Bank for three reasons. Firstly, it is a major and historic, a legendary, Newfoundland fishing harbour: we had never been there by sea and we had friends there to boot. Secondly, it was Sam's hometown. Thirdly, if somewhat romantically, it was where our great grandfather, (Philip's and mine) the Reverend John Pratt had preached his last sermon, and died in 1904. That was well before our father, John Kerr Pratt, or we were born. But for whatever reason, most likely out of general fatigue, we had given up on that by the time we had come abeam of Brunette. Allowing that we could sail around to Grand Bank from Conception Bay anytime we wanted a four or five day cruise, we bore off 90 degrees to round the tip of the Burin Peninsula and cross Placentia Bay.

By the time we entered the tickle that separates Newfoundland from St. Pierre – Canada from France – it was dark and the wind had gone very light. We lowered the main sail and jib and started the motor. What wind there was had backed around to the south-southeast, bringing the fog in with it, but navigation is generally easier and more accurate under power than under sail. We were able to identify the lights as we rounded Point May, and take a bearing on and a distance off the light on Allan's Island. So, we set a course toward Cape St. Mary's: 120 degrees magnetic, allowing for sea-room and leeway. The wind freshened for an hour or so, getting up a bit of a lop where the tide was running against it coming out along the western shore of Placentia Bay. It then moderated to a light five- to ten-knot breeze, so we hoisted sail again – a full main with a medium-sized working jib.

We were keeping two-man, six-hour watches. I was on the 'graveyard watch' – midnight to 6 a.m. – when we hardened up close-hauled on starboard tack to sail across the wide open mouth of Placentia Bay. The wind stayed light, just a draft really, but enough to keep us whispering along at a steady 5 knots. We crossed a calm rippling sea, riding a hypnotic rhythm of long ocean swells coming at us from the open North Atlantic, in and out of the fog banks, but never completely clear of it. I was alone on deck on the wheel around 4:30 a.m., just coming on daylight, when I heard someone singing "Let Me Fish off Cape St. Mary's." It seemed to be coming from the stern in a strange, distant, echoing voice. "Take me back to my western boat": it was quite magical. Then it became a choir of voices, as if there were dory-loads of singers hidden in the fog all around us. "Let me see my dory lift." The magic grew into a sense of joy, of elation. Then, my watch mate, Dick, the ship's doctor, who had been below making coffee and preparing breakfast for the oncoming watch, stuck his Afro up through the companion way and said, "My God, Chris boy, you're in fine voice this morning." The singing had stopped with the sight of him. He handed me a strong cup of coffee and proceeded to explain to me that a combination of fatigue and the gentle, rhythmic motion of the boat, the gurgling, millions of bubbles breaking hiss of the water slipping past the transom, the sleepy, somnambulant silence of being under sail had caused me to hallucinate. I accept but do not always welcome scientific explanations for what might otherwise be magic. So we talked about that and agreed there were many things resistant to analysis, and one of them would always be the question, "Why?" The new watch came on deck and it being the tradition, I told the new helmsman how the wind had been and what course I had steered overnight. No one had to remind us to watch and listen for ships entering or leaving that great fishing and increasingly industrialized bay. The wind bore further into the south but it was still soft. We held the 120-degree course. Then there was a break in the fog and the watch called, "Cape St. Mary's fine on the port bow." We all went up to have a look; what else would sailors do? I returned to the 'magic' word: obviously I had held steady on the course all the while, according to the doctor, I was "hallucinating." "Explain that to me," says I, knowing perfectly well that in those conditions, and many others, this fine little C&C sloop could sail itself.

∾

We had sailed from Allan's Island to Mistaken Point without changing tack. It was foggy all the way. The wind stayed light and continued veering into the south and finally southwest until it went flat altogether. As we drifted past a shoal of rocks off Pt. Lance – the "Bull and Cow and the Calf" – we fired up the diesel again and wound up motoring from there to Cappahayden.

The hours at sea from Allan's Island to Cappahayden were the most satisfying of the trip, visually and spiritually. An experience I felt had been a gift to me. The fog had thinned to a mist as we passed Cape St. Mary's and then lifted for an hour or so, and we crossed the mouth of St. Mary's Bay under a fine late afternoon sky. I know the land there: I could see the southern end of Great Colinet Island and Point La Haye up in the Bay, and we were able to pass close-by Cape English. Seaward, the subtle but massive groundswell was made visually palpable by the texture of the ripples on the water. That became an ironic reminder of the essential flatness of the ocean. Off St. Vincent's beach and Peter's River, whales blew and sounded and passed under the boat. There were always assemblies of shearwaters, gulls on the surface, and gannets diving everywhere. Abeam of St. Shott's, the pale blue-green of the sea darkened into indigo as the fog rolled in again. Before we crossed Trepassey Bay it engulfed Cape Pine, but its foghorn, which hadn't bothered to quit in the brief hours of clearing, continued to remind us where we were.

That night we worked our way around Cape Race in fog and total darkness. There was a report of some icebergs three miles off the Cape, so we were concerned with staying inside a three-mile perimeter, where it was very still, allowing us to get safely close to shore. There was zero visibility. As we crept along, we turned the engine off from time to time to listen for the foghorn, which in the end was very close. In that silence, we entered a strange, unreal, almost dreamlike world with very little spatial reference. All the signs were sounds, except the signs of our own small ship: the running lights at the bow glowing in a small cocoon of fog, the red light from the compass card glowing on the helmsman's face and the white stern light like a huge firefly, abaft the backstay.

On the boat, it was always a luxury to see the day go around. All hours, all twenty-four belonged to us. There was no hierarchy of obligation ordering us away from any discriminated-against time of day. We were as round as the days themselves. Midnight passed on the same smooth arc as midday. How fair, how reasonable it was to be permitted sleep by day and save, 'lay away,' some waking hours for the night.

It can be very strange at sea in the water-level cockpit of a small sailboat on a dark foggy night. You can lose your vertical as well as your horizontal orientation. In calm conditions, with no horizon anywhere, it can be very difficult to see, even to know, where the surface is. You feel the 'ups' more than the 'downs' as the boat rides over the swells. You get the impression that you are going up and up, and that the surface of the sea may be a hundred feet below you. So you look over the transom where the stern light augments the glow of phosphorescent creatures in its wake, and toward the bow where the running lights reflect in the water for reassurance. We were like a ship floating in space. We could hear the birds on the water: awkward, unmelodic, alien, not like the songbirds on land. We were in a place, a time, not natural for our kind, our species. As we rounded north, the fog began to lift and we could see the great Cape Race light – first as a rising, falling, sweeping glow, then suddenly as a cold green fire brilliant through the night. With daylight, the wind came up and we hoisted sails and rolled and romped northward past Renews, Ferryland ... Bay Bulls, Cape Spear and finally rounded Cape St. Francis into Conception Bay. We were full of enthusiasm for what boating gave us: the sense and knowledge of being offshore, of being in a strange and haunted place, of being Newfoundlanders and coming home to our land across water.

Back in my studio in Salmonier, I wanted to make a painting that would celebrate what I had seen and experienced, what the trip had been. I would call it *Land Across Water*. But as I tried to come to grips with getting back to work, with making something, a souvenir of what I'd seen and where I'd been, I had to fight with my distractions and find a new discipline. In that working part of my life, the boating becomes a distraction, a contradiction. I can't survive unless I give my work complete attention, an undistracted application of my means. And so the circle goes around and I know again that reality is one thing, but making art of it is another: a different kind of voyage.

On Dry Fly, 1976

1988
Phantom Traveler

It is the sixth morning of hard frost in a row, overcast and -12 degress. The pond is completely frozen. The arc of the ice-edge is creeping down river and along the banks at the running-out. The people with Ski-Doos, who often have to wait until February for snow on the Avalon Peninsula, must be in their glory, together with the outfits that sell the roaring machines and attendant gear.

We had access to one of the first primitive Ski-Doos on the island back around 1970. J.C. Pratt and Company sold them for awhile, but Dad gave up on it because they were in constant need of servicing. He didn't want to get into the garage "racket," much less cope with the constant complaints. At that time, they looked to him like playthings for the rich. Perhaps he misjudged the potential market and didn't foresee that every second Newfoundlander would be willing to 'sell the house' to get one and the in-country access and freedom they provided. More likely, he was getting tired of business. In 1972, Philip came home from architecture school at UBC and set up in practice. Dad saw the writing on the wall, the absence of succession, and sold J.C. Pratt and Company in 1974.

I experienced a few hours of backcountry (not very far back) freedom on that loud, yellow, gassy-smelling machine. On one occasion, I rode into Murphy's River overloaded with Fred Clarke on the back. Coming out we broke through the ice, in the shallows at the edge of Labyrinth Pond. Fortunately, we were not out in the middle or we might have been among the first recorded casualties. Fred went to his armpits in mud and slush and got wet through. I stayed dry, lifting myself up at the front end where the skis and engine remained sticking into the air. We managed to get it out, started, and rode it home, but Fred got a bad cold out of it and later shingles. I don't think he ever fully recovered from that, having one health crisis after another until he died in 1979. That was the last time I was ever on a 'ski-doo' or an ATV for that matter.

Of course, I also took the kids for short, safe rides. Once or twice, I went with Donna across the pond and upriver as far as Sandy Point, by way of the ancient river course – an alder-flat crossed here and there by the hummock remains of old beaver dams and houses. In retrospect, that was all innocent enough, but it gave rise to my reference to a "phantom traveler," real or otherwise, in things I wrote about in later years.

1991
The Stamp Prints

I made the stamp prints as souvenirs of Newfoundland: not Newfoundland as an island – its fauna and geography – but as a social, political, economic entity that has passed out of time. These early postage stamps constitute evidence of that Newfoundland.

In my prints, the subjects are all actual Newfoundland postage stamps, dating from 1865 to 1887, enlarged approximately twenty times. They are not, however, photographic enlargements. The images as I printed them are not at all the same in texture or in detail as they would be if they were direct photographic blow-ups. In making the stencils for the prints, I tried to put myself in the role of the original engraver, and using the actual stamps as models, I proceeded to make the stencil as finely as I could. Therefore, for example, the lettering and the curves and scrimshaw around the pictorial subject matter are much sharper, and more even and controlled than they would have been in facsimile enlargements of the original engravings. Such enlargements would have magnified the rough and ragged edges left by the engraving tool, even in the hands of the most skilled engraver, working in such a minute format as a postage stamp.

Making these prints was something of a busman's holiday for me. I rarely use lettering in my work, and never much resembling decoration, but I enjoy doing both. Making the stamp prints gave me a chance to do these things while avoiding the aesthetic responsibility. I was working my hand around what had been someone else's design. Collectively and individually, these prints also relate to stamp collecting, which has interested me off and on since I was a boy.

1991

The way the tide came surging into the river this morning, breaking up the ice and heaving it up on the lawn, reminded me of a time years ago. John and I were sitting on the living room floor, soaking off stamps and arranging them in sets, when the roar of a similar tide startled us. We looked up to see jagged shards of ice rafting against the fence, smashing it into kindling.

My own introduction to stamp collecting began when I would 'help' my father soak Newfoundland stamps off envelopes he had brought home from the office. He was an avid collector and lover of all things concerning Newfoundland. I printed *1887 10¢ Black* as a block-of-nine mural for installation in the new offices of J.C. Pratt and Co. Ltd. in St. John's, which he built in 1969. It was a surprise to him and he was quite emotional when I unveiled it in my studio. I don't think he realized how much I respected what he had achieved.

1991

Space can serve as an equivalent for time in visual art: near being now and far either past or future. I like juxtapositions of near and far, of deep and shallow space: the boards almost at the picture plane, the shallow recess of the blind behind the window frame and suddenly the sea, back to infinity. There isn't any middle ground, no transition, only here and there, now and then. I liked getting depth without recourse to diagonals, without disappearing railway tracks and avenues of wire poles. I preferred the space described by overlapping planes, defined by vertical and horizontal lines.

Those preoccupations led me to an image where things seemed to be waiting or on hold, so I called it *Sunday Afternoon*.

1991

In a landscape where there is very little sign of spring, Easter is an empty time of year. We have Easter without daffodils, a few crocuses maybe, but no convincing show of resurrection from the land itself. The land looks spent and flayed. Some years it is easy to believe that nothing will ever grow again.

I wanted to do an Easter print, and I was working toward an image with the *Good Friday* title in mind. I kept remembering how pale and shadowless the sunlight was, and how reassuring and secure the wooden houses looked.

1991

I really enjoy painting on large canvasses. In some ways Mount Allison in the late '50s was a bit of a waste of time: no models, no sculpture, no graphic arts except silkscreen ...

I envied the scale and bravado, the technical gymnastics I saw in the work of the best senior students at Glasgow. I was starting to be uncomfortable with working on a small scale, and, although I admired what other artists achieved using egg tempera on small, classically gessoed boards, I worried that, in my hands, it might become overly precious, appropriate to people of few and limited ideas who needed time and technical obsessions to flesh them out: that I would be seen cracking eggs and mixing powdered pigments from little cosmetic bottles as if that alchemy would somehow make an otherwise indifferent image into art. Of course, no one ever suggested we should do that. It was an anxiety of my own.

I often ask myself why I quit the meat and muscle, the challenges of the Glasgow School of Art. There seemed to be good reasons at the time, but perhaps it was a matter of immaturity, of insecurity. Or have the obvious benefits of being at Mount Allison in the late '50s outweighed that?

1992
At Mt. Allison

Things went well yesterday. There were a lot of people at the talk, but there aren't many of the old guard left. Forty years is a long time in the life of an individual, if only an atom in the history of the race and a quark in the history of time. Despite some major surgery a couple of years ago, Ted Pulford, one of that few, looks much better, much healthier, than most. We had dinner with him and June. Afterwards, because it was too early to commit to the discomforts of the motel's brick bed or confine my outlook to that small, claustrophobic room, we drove through the dark night over to Dorchester. Although it is much built up, there are still many isolated, dilapidated houses, looking damp and musty and more than ever haunted by a past in which small farming held some promise.

Sackville has grown a lot also, with housing spreading over areas that forty years ago were farmland. There are new buildings at the university, but most of the downtown changes are just a change of face and function. The Tribune building, the Paper Box Company and the building that was the Steadman stores remain, looking like details from early Colvilles. The old buildings are very recognizable behind the new façades and some have not changed at all. Mel's seems to have the same bottles of maple syrup in the window as it did in 1953. Looking through that window, I would have sworn the proprietor was the original Mel, miraculously preserved, immunized against the ravages of time, but surely, it was his son or grandson. The Sackville Harness shop now sells fancy, up-market cowboy boots. Some of the older wooden buildings have had restoration facelifts that seem inspired by what Philip has initiated in St. John's. A few, like 'The Barn,' have been torn down.

One of the things that driving around these old haunts reveals is the considerable distances we walked – miles and miles and miles. I can only wonder what we talked about: little of substance, much of wishful thinking or rhetoric and homesickness on my part. Mary says we fought a lot: the walks were long enough to allow the tensions of insecurity to build to silence but leave time for a rush of reconciliation before getting back to the college residences.

My sleep was a river of strange dreams: there was the usual 'big boat' dream somewhere – I retain that only as a flavour. Then I was wandering in strange rooms full of abandoned junk, looking for privacy, and that became a dream about old friends and affections. Then I was driving over a very rough road (inspired by the driving earlier yesterday out to the Jolicure Lakes) and turned around in haste when an immense sand storm loomed ahead of us (Ted Pulford had been talking about the war in North Africa over dinner at Bordens). I also had a dream that I was soon to die voluntarily, and the realization that I was reasonably healthy and not old enough for that, and a decision not to let it be, woke me up.

So today I go to talk to the students at the Fine Arts School. I have no eye for age; the students don't look all that different from their teachers to me. I remember being here myself but, oddly, I have to be reminded that two of our children are now graduates. I run into professors who remember them. It is a very wet, cold, dreary day in Sackville. I would like to go out for a brisk walk. I won't let the weather rule it out.

1992

From my bedroom window on LeMarchant Road, I could see St. John's Harbour across the roofs and chimney pots of Cabot Street. To the east, the narrows opened St. John's to the sea and to the world. To the west, I could see Waterford Valley, where the trains escaped the town. They traveled, in my mind, through unspoiled country thick with caribou and ptarmigan, past lakes and rivers full of trout and climbed the wild, barren Topsails before descending to the West Coast and the Gulf, to meet the boats that went to Canada. That was my version of the romance of trains enriched by the poetry of place names, stations on the line: Wreckhouse, Mizzen Topsail, Kitty's Brook, Placentia Junction, Fox Marsh Siding ....

1992

St. John's is still a wooden town. It was all but destroyed by fire twice; the third great fire is under way, piecemeal, three houses at a time. Although there are still well-preserved houses, the slums of St. John's Centre are long gone, their structures bulldozed by developers, their people moved elsewhere. Less than fifty years ago there were still areas of squalor: moldering wooden houses with little heat and no running water, relieved by night-soil carts. *St. John's Centre* is a neat, formal drawing of an environment that was neither neat nor formal, and the painting that grew out of it acknowledges no more than the romantic memory of the smell of burning coal. Is that an impertinence – to reduce ugly realities to considered textures on a plane? Reality, with its ragged-arsed imperatives, confronts and slaps me in the face, but order whispers in my ear and like a wicked messenger gains my confidence.

1992

I went out to Bay Roberts last night to discuss the launching of the Heritage Society poster with the committee members. They are all well-gotten-out, civilized, civic-minded people. They represent a kind of society that is more well-to-do and less burdened with doctrine and superstition than our neighbours in St. Mary's Bay. Had we moved to Brigus or Bay Roberts instead of here, we would have had our relatives and old friends as neighbours but they could not have been more friendly or helpful than our neighbours here. Yet life would have been very different, especially for Mary: there would have been a Protestant church she could go to. I talked a lot about Ocean Pond and old friends in Bay Roberts, perhaps making too much of it. However, the fact that my memory of those days is vivid must be evidence of a power, an influence that would be hard for me to overstate, that has provided me with many images.

That is one past, littered with people, places and incidents, rich in dark Victoriana, the erotica of art deco and the exciting circumstantial voyeurism of being a child, a fly on the wall, not credited with awareness and insight. It is a past now haunted with memories of tensions and anxieties, of weaknesses and jealousies, some of which became my own. It is a memory of dark rooms.

My memories of the Southern Avalon are of another past: Trepassey, Southeast Placentia and the Cape Shore, Big Barachois and Little Salmonier. These are open, fresh-air memories of minimally furnished, undecorated rooms with bright pearly sunlight filtered through the fog and windows whose access to the sea and sky was not compromised by overhanging trees. These are memories of houses standing unsheltered on the open land, of brooks and estuaries where no one lived at all. I didn't know the people there, I had no relatives, and no friends or even contacts my own age, no roots, and no access to the lives and attitudes of that society. We were always paying guests at the hotel. Later, when we built the cabin on the Southeast River and I worked at the Base, I learned a little more, but not in a visceral way.

I live in a valley, not on a headland – I walk around my garden here at Salmonier or along the riverbank looking down the valley to the south and west and see the sun setting over Hurley's Bridge and beyond that the Western Shore. I get unacceptably romantic about it all: it seems to me that the wind blowing in my face is blowing from the past, that on its way upriver it has seen evidence and ghosts of us fishing at Big Barachois and bears the flavour of that evidence.

1992

It's nearly nine o'clock. Things are tense today – the business of total togetherness again. I dislike the "we" in my professional life, but it is always there, or so my short fuse indicates. I need to spend time alone, and when circumstances deliver solitude, I enjoy it very much. If not solitude, then silence for a large part of the day with the option to come and go and do things unannounced, without censure, actual or implied; to have equal access to the past, present and future without road blocks in any direction.

1992

The river is very low, even for August. I have seen a couple of trout jump, or at least seen the rings, but the pond seems dead. The birds are no longer singing in chorus at dawn and, of course, the night winnowing snipe are silent now. I am cresting the summer's hill, staring blindly into the long, lonely valley of fall. Behind me, way down the valley, is the distant past, seen over other more recent things. It seems to be the wide, wet, wind-lit marshlands of the Tantramar, open and echoing, hollow, haunted, distant like the distant land in Brueghel's paintings. And there are Brueghel-like figures in the distance there: a mixed up, angry young man – moody, manipulative, selfish and jealous – and an attractive, intelligent and passionate young woman. He knows that he is the dependent one, that he will wait for her where the foundry track branches off the main CN line. Perhaps she is crying as he stomps on ahead of her, not wanting her to know that she could destroy him by not following, by just turning to walk the other way.

Tantramar Marshes: The Highmarsh Road

1993

It is a fall day. I have the feeling that I am setting out to walk to the Glasgow School of Art, my portfolio under my arm, brown and golden leaves beneath my feet. The low, waning sun, reaching through an uncommonly thin smog that shrouds the Kelvin River valley, casts a distant warmth on my right cheek. I am young, my step is quick, but I am already aware that nothing will come easily, that I must not let down my guard. Happiness is for me as veiled, thin and remote as the sun's warmth on my cheek, not filling me up or enveloping me, not present everywhere. Alone in a strange and interesting place, my eyes turn inward, homeward. Already I walk through avenues of memory and inhabit a landscape of the mind. Who waits for me back home? Why is everything so unresolved? Do I see that everything will remain elusive, distant and ultimately unattainable?

A friend told me once that my mother had, with respect to my work and career, repeated: "None of this comes easily to Christopher."

1993
Toronto

Last night, Mira and I ate at a restaurant whose name escapes me now. It was just the two of us. The food was very good but it was quite noisy and very busy. I found it hard to hear Mira as her voice does not carry well. I find it interesting to talk to her about her European background and experiences and get the ins and outs of the really big leagues: her encounters and friendships with major artists, dealers and collectors and people who knew the likes of Matisse and Picasso. It must be frustrating for her to be the owner of a gallery where a painter of my limitations counts as one of the 'stars.' She has the challenge of convincing people that I am the real thing and getting the relatively modest prices (relative to real, international stars) she does for my work. For my part, I do the best I can, but maybe not the best I could have done had I chosen to guts-it-out, living somewhere else, and risked trying to survive the whirlpools in the mainstream.

1993

I have seen hundreds of moose on the roads in Newfoundland over the years. I have seen them caught in the glare of oncoming trucks, silhouetted, their dark bodies steaming. What I remember is their obvious bewilderment, fright and seeming paralysis in the face of it: the insecurity of having a strange, hard surface underfoot, the blinding lights, the noise and chaos. Those were the origins of the *Moose and Transports* painting. I liked the word transport in lieu of truck, associating it in this context with Emily Dickinson's use of it in her poem, "A Narrow Fellow in the Grass."

Artists who use subject matter cannot expect to have their work assessed based on abstract or aesthetic properties alone; they want the impact and connections inherent in recognition, and they have to risk having the wrong connections made. They walk the line, asking to have it both ways, and frequently they cannot. All of it is inconsequential if the images fail, if they cannot stand on their own feet as messengers, if they don't achieve another dimension.

I have seen moose shot 50 feet from my studio: like animals on night roads – they just stood there while bullets smacked into them, rippling their flanks, confused, transfixed and terrified.

Moose crossing Salmonier River by the studio window

1994
Red Fox

It is a grey morning with snowflakes swirling around my studio windows. The wind is brisk upriver. The pond, but not the river, is frozen and white with snow: the silver-grey water beats against its greenish-yellow edge. The forest is a dark, rich, winter green.

My studio is empty, except for its furnishings – no work. I have come here to try to work after nearly four months of not doing anything. I have tried before and failed, spending my time sitting at my drafting table, as I am doing now, watching the river and the wilderness, listening to liturgical music.

A red fox lopes out of the forest, runs along the pond edge, checking a scent as it goes, then disappears into the woods again. A hundred feet further along a mink emerges from under the ice and makes for the woods as well. Is it the fox's quarry, or is this a coincidence? I have seen foxes here before. I decided some time ago to consider the unexpected appearance of an animal to be a good omen. The passage of a caribou through the garden ten years ago, in 1984, seemed to precede a change in my outlook and fortunes. I am about to ask if the fox is such a sign, if it somehow atones me for killing the beaver that was destroying the trees in our garden, when, looking up the pond I see the fox out on the ice investigating the now unoccupied beaver's house. I am depressed and I have this hateful, tired ache in my stomach. So I ask, instead, do these signs mean that since I killed the beaver, animals will not be a party to my psychology any more? A half-hour later, the fox, probably starving, is still patrolling the edge.

I could have written all of this thirty years ago. The winter world has changed less than the summer world. My objectives as a painter were different then. That was the first stage, the pre-Mira stage. Newfoundland was still Newfoundland in my mind: we still salted fish, skiffs still rode to moorings in the harbours, immense shoals of caplin still rolled ashore every June, we still drove on dirt roads and took the train to Corner Brook. Then there was the middle period, the time of accelerated success and the unconscious establishment of a product line, a 'look' that culminated in the Vancouver retrospective in 1985.

I found images within that doctrine that were meaningful to me. I wanted to do more, and there were more to do, but I needed a fresh start, so, finally, in 1989, I built a new studio. The momentum and enthusiasm that engendered ended when it was destroyed by fire fourteen months after I started working there. The sense of loss and futility that followed was reflected in some of the paintings I did then: *Room at St. Vincent's*; *Moose and Transports*; *Freight Shed*. But now it is the final period and it cannot be like the others. Perhaps I should have done more, but whatever got in the way, indolence maybe, I did not. With *Freight Shed*, that middle period is over. Times have changed, tastes have changed and I have changed. What was not done will not be done, its time has gone. Mary moved into St. John's to live and work two years ago and I am here alone, free to work and wander without compromise. What will be done demands and will have its own time.

It is brighter, looks as if the brisk west wind may bring clearing. The fox seems to be gone. I am now listening to Gregorian chant, its hollow, echoing sound reminds me as much of the empty hangars and bunkers of Argentia as it does of the great cathedrals or monasteries of Europe. I have seen the first, but imagine the second. It's time to find my way again.

1994

A mild winter morning, but nothing is melting. Sunlight comes and goes with passing clouds. Light strikes silver on the open water. The fox appeared again, following the same pattern as yesterday. I am playing liturgical music and looking through my lists again. But looking through and refining lists is not making things and I will not be back at work until I make things – but what things to make?

John made paintings of birds and plants, but his picture-making grew out of his preoccupation with natural history and had little to do with ART.

Barby asked me one day out of the blue if I had a canvas she could use. She had never painted before, but what emerged was an image of astounding technical and aesthetic sophistication and originality.

Ned carved wooden models and did daydream drawings of boats, but when he went beyond that I could see in his pictures an adventurous, off-center inventiveness that required only confidence to bloom into something very special.

Anne was determined to opt out of the family trade, except that writing was also a traditional Pratt family trade. Her penchant was for criticism and I often reminded her – as Churchill is said to have observed – that in all the history of man no statue had ever been erected to a critic. I also repeated the old saying that it is a lot easier to criticize than to do.

So she came into my studio and commandeered an already primed board. Then, leafing nonchalantly through one of several Skira art books Mary and I bought with wedding present money, settled on *Corot's Bridge at Nantes*, and got to doing a copy of it. Using oil paints, sight unassisted, she finished that in a couple of hours, daubed in the guy's red hat with a flourish and said "There." And that was it; she never painted again. From three feet away it would be hard to tell it from the original. Checkmate!

John, 1976

1997

Pastel-coloured boulders, rounded and shining, based with darker browns and blackish greens remind me of the boulders in Edvard Munch. That observation now reminds me of how Michael Snow and Joyce Weiland laughed so dismissively when they visited Salmonier many years ago. Driving them through the Mt.Carmel/Harricott/Colinet loop, I observed a disposition of buildings, grasses and meadows all in a light that I said reminded me of Corot. Corot! Oh, what a laugh that was.

1997

I don't believe art has much political clout in any positive sense. Political content or agenda is a waste of time at best and at worst a cop out. It is too frequently neo-romanticism, easy, automatic content, modern purple prose. If you want to be overtly political there is the art of politics itself, the ultimate participatory art in a democracy, the ultimate 'happening.' That should be your medium. The great German painters, musicians and writers didn't prevent Hitler; Tolstoy, Dostoevsky and Tchaikovsky didn't prevent Stalin and Goya's *Disasters* didn't prevent the Spanish Civil War. Picasso's *Guernica* didn't stop one bomb from dropping or influence World War ll. In fact, it is more interesting as a painting and a key to Picasso's formal innovations, as art not politics. Sadly, music and images are used more effectively as instruments of propaganda and hate than as advocates of peace.

With John Carter and prototype Newfoundland and Labrador flag, 1980

1997

We drove out to Corner Brook on Monday to be at Grenfell College when George Maslov gets at printing *Two Dories Once*. I have told Memorial that we will aim for an edition of forty-five, plus the usual shop and printer's copies and maybe ten artist's proofs for my personal use. The edition – all forty-five of them, will be my contribution to the anniversary fund, a donation, free and clear, and they are free to do with them what they will. I assumed they would put the prints on the market, but apparently they have decided to give a 'thank-you' copy of the lithograph to anyone who makes a donation of a yet to be determined amount. Actually, there's some dignity in that.

Despite being a Master Printer, George doesn't have a shop assistant and has to do all the preparation, cleanup and general grunge work himself, which is an unfortunate waste of his time. So Jeanette came with me to pitch in and learn something about the process. She got the hang of it quickly and has been a great help. Twelve years of working with me on silkscreen prints has given her a lot of shop smarts. But she also came along for the ride, and to help with the driving while I made notes triggered by associations with the places we were passing through, all of them new to her. Her enthusiasm for all of it was infectious and her response to the picnic and pitstop places where I stopped, out of long and memorable habit, brought new life to them.

We're asked to a house party tomorrow night but, with respect, we're going to drive up the Great Northern Peninsula instead. I haven't been north of Port aux Choix since 1971. I would like to get as far as Ferolle Point, just north of the Highlands of St. John and Castors River at the southeast entrance to the Strait of Belle Isle – the first place you can see the coast of Labrador, continental North America, from sea level. We'll be late getting back to the inn tonight, but we have to be up early and on our way home to St. Mary's Bay tomorrow.

1998

I drafted a letter many months ago when I had just started working on the Deer Lake painting. For some reason the letter didn't get sent. It said, in part: I am doing a painting – 45 inches x 10 feet long – of the Deer Lake powerhouse, all those wonderful windows at night and the fury of the water escaping from the penstocks. I may call it *Junction Brook Memorial* if I decide to be political. Actually, that says it all.

In the first instance, it proceeds from that wonder we share at the immense power of water. Then, at least for me, a kind of revulsion at its entrapment, its imprisonment behind dams and containment in penstocks and the fury of its release, like a wild horse breaking the gates, illustrating the historical appropriateness of the concept of horsepower.

A few miles east of Deer Lake, the Trans-Canada Highway crosses the dry riverbed of what was once a major river connecting the extensive drainage basin of the Grand Lake, Sandy Lake, Birchy Lake watersheds to the Humber River, in western Newfoundland. It is called, modestly, Junction Brook. Where the road crosses a bridge immediately below Deer Lake power station, you become aware that the first has become the second. Salmon still muzzle into the tailrace, still trying to access their ancient spawning grounds upstream that have been dry for over seventy years. Junction Brook, now just a string of beaver gullies connected by trickles of water, is still posted as a salmon stream – "fly-fishing only" – a pretense that life still goes on.

But life does go on, the forces of nature become the implements of art. Built in the early 1920s, the powerhouse itself (a functional Parthenon in the wilds of Newfoundland), elegant and expressive in its architecture, becomes a secular cathedral. Its interior is not dark; its windows do not embellish and admit light and the enlightenment of day through coloured glass into an otherwise sepulchral interior. The light comes from the inside out; the brilliance and variety of the windows speak of the achievements of man, not the glory of God. The building hums with potential and throbs with vitality, not with choirs singing and the boom of a pipe organ.

Which is where it all 'comes round': the organ and the choir, the great cathedrals, the concept and the rationalization of God in art are the issues of human achievement as well. The water that raged out of the generators is absorbed into the placid waters of Deer Lake itself, a hundred yards below the bridge. Anglers in chest-waders wade out to their armpits to practice the abstract art of fishing for salmon with artificial flies, and catch them there.

I don't often paint actual places or things. Art is not reality, but often reality is art. For me, driving across what now remains of Junction Brook and re-encountering it at Deer Lake has a complex aesthetic about it that I struggle to describe. It is a conceptual experience. As a painter, all I could celebrate was light.

1999

A sense of place is very important in my work, especially in its development, even if, as is usually the case, the final image does not represent any particular location. I spend a lot of time, days or weeks, focused on my preliminary drawings as if they were Rorschach blots asking, "Where is this, what season is it, what kind and time of day is it?"

I knew where the Trout River paintings came from, and that it was winter. I had first been in the Trout River hills – as we called them then – in 1956, well before there was any thought of that seemingly desolate landscape ever becoming a national park. I have been there in winter when the winds are so high and the blizzards so blinding it is impossible to know where you are. Even experienced heavy equipment operators have found themselves turned around, heading in the wrong direction, when trying to clear the road through Trout River Gulch. And in years past, the doctor traveling on foot from Winter House Brook to Trout River village could often only find his way by following the telegraph poles along the margins of the Old Mail Road.

I go there in all seasons and weathers and hike as high as I can, to the edge of my nerve more than the limit of my endurance. That is high enough to know that it is a place as treacherous and formidable as it is magnificent. I have been there in torrential rainstorms and watched water streaming off the Tablelands, as it would off the backs of surfacing whales, only to disappear into the rubble and scree. Even the larger brooks go underground. It is easy to imagine that the whole system is still in motion, afloat on a bed of silt, a residue of its geological origins. The moraines and fans of rubble look as if they happened yesterday. There is always evidence of continuous shift and even boulders as big as refrigerators sometimes rattle underfoot. You feel that you are disturbing a living thing and that the whole mountain could come crashing down on you like a giant 2000-foot wave.

Jeanette and I spent several truly wonderful days roaming around in the Trout River hills last August. One warm evening, we sat on a boulder in the scree 500 feet above Berry Barren Brook, watching the sunset paint the hills: first orange then red through purple to black, in a rare silence in which the insects buzzing and the chickadees calling from low thickets of dwarf junipers became spots of violet and gold on an otherwise white page. On other occasions, we hiked deep into the Dry Brook and Winter House Brook canyons when it was warm and dry and the naked rock and rubble – dark green serpentine and ancient peridotite oxidized to a sulphurous yellow – seemed more like Arizona than a sub-arctic environment. Yet, there was evidence everywhere that the 27-degree temperatures of those summer afternoons would drop to -30 on winter nights. The signature of ancient and recent winters still prevailed and pockets of snow still lingered in the deeper crevices on the north face of the Tablelands.

When we left for Trout River, the paintings were in my studio 'roughed-in,' predominantly whitish-grey boards with darker shades emerging, suggesting bushes and rocks and promontories, as much paintings of a blizzard as a place. When I returned to my studio with the hills fresh in my mind, I started to recognize or imagine actual features in the sketches I had made from memory years ago, and to identify them with 'real' places. That strengthened my sense of place, the feeling, as I was working, that I was there in a literal as well as a spiritual sense. In those brief weeks of welcome and accessibility, it was as if the place had bared its soul to me: hard, weathered, beautiful, come from the sea, older than the continent itself – a metaphor for the planet, for the universe, for Newfoundland.

With respect to the Trout River pictures, my original idea was to do one large painting, provisionally titled *Blizzard in the Trout River Hills*. I spent a very dramatic day there about twelve years ago, not expecting the blizzard that often obscured the road and made it dangerous, when I got out, to venture more than a few yards from the car. It was a gale-driven blizzard, not actually snowing most of the time, so there were occasional glimpses of the sun, giving me the impression that I was able to see more above me than on either side. The vertical shape of the paintings is a result of a requirement for focus, a sense of place. I felt that sense of place most strongly when I tried, instinctively, this essentially non-landscape format. Perhaps that can be rationalized in terms of a sense of height and vertical distance, the straight-line distance from my feet to the top of the hills and the urge I always feel to climb and find out what is at the top.

At the top of the Tablelands, 2001

1999

My home is located on the estuary of the Salmonier River at the height of tide, the farthest inland reach of St. Mary's Bay. Precisely where the river and the estuary meet there is a pond where the flood tides of winter hurl the bay ice crashing against the river ice. The pond is a sanctuary where the returning geese rest and feed in spring, before the ice has melted off their inland nesting ponds, and where the trout and salmon wait for the river to reach that taste and temperature which summons them to the spawning rituals of fall. The pond is also a haven and a hideout for everything that hunts and devours the fish and their progeny: osprey, mergansers, kingfishers, loons, otters and seals. And, once upon a time, me.

My studio overlooks this pond but I have never painted it. I have watched it, day in, day out, in all moods and weathers for thirty-seven years and I never tire of it. Its ebb and flow have timed my life; its seasons have been my metronome. I know when to expect the geese, to watch for the otter's young and listen for snipe winnowing. I know when I'll have to endure the blessedly brief tourist season and the city anglers and that I'll have to complain again to a deaf authority about the presence of voracious harbour seals. I know, as the seals know, where the trout and salmon lie.

Here, the habits of *Salmo salar* and *Salmo trutta*, cousins though they be, are not the same. The salmon are always on the move, unable to still that restlessness which returns them to the rivers where they were born after a thousand-mile journey to the shrimp pastures of the Labrador Sea. To live is to move: I see them in perpetual motion just below the surface of the pond, moving through the thick, brackish water as effortlessly as if theirs was a continuum of transubstantiation. Even their leaping is purposeful, directional.

Like an older, wiser species, the big anadromous brown trout find a comfortable "lie" and stay there, knowing that their time will come; they cannot rush it. They jump straight up at predictable intervals, always in the same place, as if it were an obligation and not an enthusiasm.

That is not to say they enjoy or tolerate a hook in their jaw. I don't fish much anymore, but when I do, I fish for trout; and when they are hooked, they fight. Sometimes, as I back away from my work, to clean a brush or find a new one, I notice from my studio window that a good trout is showing at one of the stations of the pond. Over the years, these stations have acquired names: the Corner, the Cove, the Old Block, the Bull Tow, the Canal. I will watch him (large trout are always him), maybe for a week, sometimes two. Then, of an evening, something will take hold of me and I will find myself picking up my old cane rod, rowing out to where I can cast for him, park my ancient rowboat in the reeds and time his rise.

I am, of course, a traditionalist: I will have tied on a small dry fly, a 'standard' pattern – a Royal Coachman or a Queen of the Waters or a Dark Montreal. If it is a calm night, the viscous fall water may still show the bubbles of his previous surfacing. Then, at the right time, I will drop it on his spot, give the fly a little twitch, and that is it.

I never keep the fish and rarely bring it to the boat. It is all a kind of ritual, a communion – need I say that? I am the angler and the trout. I do this in remembrance of myself.

The house and studio at Salmonier, 2007

2000
Burgeo Road

Burgeo Road. A hard landscape to photograph in this flat light. The land is buried under snow. The river courses wrapped and muffled. Everything is grey and white: the sky is uniform bright grey, heightened by Naples yellow at the horizon to the south. The road has been ploughed and sanded but is covered with brown snow nonetheless. There is no wind, although wind is in the forecast. I can see it would be a difficult place in much of a wind. It would be hard to see anything, even to know that you were still on the road on the high barrens or in the funneling valleys. It is interesting in its range and distances, frightening in its potential. The right light would make subjects of the wind-sculpted snow, although this snow is so recent it still wants sculpting and texturing. The wind is beginning to rise. The Blue Hills of Couteau are already dusty, pale, smoking with drifting snow. We consider turning back. Then, suddenly, there is a shaft of light to the south over Burgeo, enticing us on into the potential whiteouts of a late return.

2000

When you revisit a place that matters to you after a long absence, it is a rich spiritual experience. However, if you then return to the place too frequently it loses some of its power. The power lies in the absences, often the absence of people you were there with before.

Went north, only past Belburns, to the brook where Dad, David Silcox, Fred Clarke and I boiled the kettle on our way to St. Anthony in 1970, thirty-one years ago. I wanted to show Jeanette the spot, but I couldn't find it. Perhaps it is under the new road. Weary of driving, we decided not to go north to Port au Choix, to walk the rocks at Pt. Riche yet again. It is a day greatly like other days I've been there, offering good old things but nothing new, although you never know what new things there may be.

We are now driving south with the sky showing overcast ahead of us and the roadside a rich potpourri of wildflowers: daisies, alizarin fireweed, red and white clover, purple vetch ... On the higher slopes of the Long Range Mountains, small patches of snow still linger in the hollows, looking like wild creatures facing extinction that have withdrawn to a distant, inaccessible shelter of their own.

2000

Burgeo Road. Heavy cloud cover and cool, thin sunlight occasionally breaking through. I have the strange feeling that it seems longer since Jeanette and I were here in June of this year than in the fall three years ago. Is this the anxiety of seeing how much change can happen in a month, or that now at the apogee of summer everything is winding down? Why do places, situations, and things seem so changed, more remote, when only recently left? Is it like the third day after a death? In visiting a place like this, is the sense of loss and change as acute and magnified as it would be by a more direct and personal loss? This sense of loss, of nostalgia – the associations that arrive from the way light or wind passes across a marsh or hills, or how something very distant arrives to knot-up in the gut – of what instinct is all that a residue: survival, love, or conscience, for that matter?

The Burgeo Road   105

2002

You can make paintings and sculptures, murals, movies, poems, performances, but you can't make art. Time and taste, fashion, insight and hindsight make art. Artists are those who, at any given time, are said by an arrangement of the elite or, very occasionally, by democratic consensus, to have made art. So it is more important to be a painter or sculptor than it is to be an artist. I am a painter, a member of a very old profession, maybe the fifth oldest after prostitutes, preachers, prophets, and profiteers, and I do what painters have always done, namely, make pictures. The pictures I make are of places I have been, in that strange space between reality and invention and, more and more, they come to represent real places, a celebration of the gift of being here, and there.

2003

Many of my most recent watercolours are about nothing more profound or significant than the pleasure and satisfaction of having been in a particular place at a particular time and the amended and simplified memory of encounters.

Naturally, you hope people who don't like your work will eventually come round to liking it, but the work itself has to accomplish that. If it does not, why should words prevail?

I take the view, which I am told is somewhat anti-intellectual, that if art is a means of communication then it ought to be capable of communicating on its own, without a lot of attendant explanation and instruction. If it really is a universal language, then more ordinary people ought to understand it than is usually the case. So I try to provide context for my offerings, but little more.

2003

Interesting things unfold as you drive at night: unexpected shapes and selections, strange colours, close visual perimeters, simplified forms and contours, mysteries, but I have no vernacular, no shorthand by which these things get translated into 'art.'

We rolled south through the night along the straight, then gently curving road, bordering the sea, Orion bright in the southern sky ahead of us, Polaris confirming north directly behind. The dark dry ribbon of pavement defined by reassuring banks of snow – our headlights opening the night ahead of us, darkness snapping shut behind us as we passed. Then the road, wide, well engineered and clean, climbed, wound through and then descended the Bonne Bay hills, exposed as if by surgery; the moraines of snow sharp against the black presence of tall, spiked spruce. It started to snow at Wiltondale. The pavement was glazed blue at first, by the thin, even white, as the first thin priming on masonite always looks blue. Then the snow deepened and the road was no longer so well defined at its edges; it was like a frozen river, its banks, still containing us, bright in our headlights. It turned into a blizzard at Deer Lake, and from Pasadena to Corner Brook, except where the road is twinned, it was tense winter driving again. There was no traffic to speak of anyway, nor had there been any on the long, lovely solitude of the Great Northern Peninsula road.

Driving to Venus From Eddie's Cove East, 2000, oil on hardboard,
private collection

2003

I got a good bit done yesterday, so it is coming along. It will need some major/minor adjustments later on. Major/minor in the sense that they may be minor in scale or scope but major in impact. As usual, I have carefully packaged and kept the paints I have been working with, which helps in the end game, and I brush in or out underpaintings for anticipated changes as I go along. Jeanette continued underpainting *Winter at Whiteway,* but she will need some focused input, mostly in the form of additional drawing, before she can continue.

I stayed at it until 8:30, when I decided I needed to go for a drive. I wound my way slowly through the night as far as Bay Roberts, where I got a large coffee and went to the banking machine. I stopped to drink my coffee on the now lonely Roaches Line, pulling over on a wide shoulder where the road crests the barrens with the moon and Mars for focal points. After I got home, I sat on the verandah in the moonlight for an hour or so. Except for the occasional car or truck, it was a very silent night: three or four fish jumped somewhere in the pond, but the snipe are gone and there were no owls or other night birds, and no frogs, not the least brush or rustle of anything alive and stirring in the woods. My mind was as blank as the night. I looked for colours, but there were none. It was black and grey and silver. The silver, especially the moon itself, could be imagined tinted with the palest orange, and the greys obtained by the mixture of deep purple and an essence of the orange diluted in the moon. The clouds seemed to be trying to get a grip on the moon, but the fingers dissolved in the effort. I thought of Dad and John as I sat on the verandah listening and looking at the pond and the moon. I could no more fix them in my thoughts than the clouds could hold the moon. For that instant, both of them seemed to have vanished from my own fleeting life to the same extent.

2003

I love this place in the morning and I get up early to be part of it. Now, at 7:15, I can see the sky clearing. A brush of rain lingers under a cloud low in the east: indigo against the pale orange band of clear sky under it. The wet, shiny bottom of the overturned aluminum boat reflects all the colours of the sky. A fall tide is pouring in, but the pond is black and calm with foam flecks picking up the light and describing its surface currents. The pre-sunrise glow is starting to pick out individual shapes and colours, and there is a little bit of mist rising off the water where Labyrinth Pond Brook enters the main river. Absurdly, there are birds singing somewhere. It sounds like spring. I go out with the binoculars to try to find out what they are, but I can see no sign of anything. They sound like siskins and seem to be in the big Norway maple by the brook. I am reminded of the siskin-like chirping I heard the night I discovered the bats in the print studio. Could they be bats settling into the tree after the night? Then, though I neither hear nor see anything fly, they sound more distant. The moose season has opened: I hear the report of a rifle, one crack only, distant, off to the north – no coup de grâce.

2003

I like being able to see the line where the land ends and the sky begins. Blizzards excite me; they have power and movement. They open and allow the skyline in and then close in again. Fog lingers, thick, lifeless unless it is in partnership with light, but somehow heavy and unsatisfactory either way. I have to overcome these jealousies, keep the horizon in my sights and find the line for myself.

Daylight reveals a sharp little breeze down the pond out of somewhere in the east. The valley, funneling, will not tell me exactly which quality of east – south or north – but portending heavy weather either way.

December 19, 2003

We went across the river and got a Christmas tree today. My sciatic hip was acting up as it often does at this time of the year, so Jeanette did most of the work. I remembered again how things like trouting or setting rabbit snares, picking berries or even the two hour expedition to find and cut down a Christmas tree got me into the country in weathers I wouldn't otherwise go in, and how different that is from a hike along a developed trail. And I remembered, as I always do, that the first girl I ever really knew died on this date in 1963 – now forty wind-borne years ago.

Life becomes a developed trail: there are unforeseen hazards – washouts, windfalls, trip-roots – but as time goes by the destination becomes clear and inevitable. Back in the summer of 1951, when she and I rode our bicycles to where the farmland became overgrown and the Old Placentia Road narrowed to a path through the second-growth – there, in that buzzing warmth of moss, meadow grass and evergreens, in the heat sink of an early August afternoon in Newfoundland, the trail was new.

Goulds farm, c. 1957

2003
Emily Christina Dawe

My earliest memory of Christmas is of my mother, Emily Christina Dawe, on one of those indistinguishable Christmases, before I was seven. Named for two maternal aunts, Christina was born on March 3, 1909, the fourteenth and youngest child of the seventeen pregnancies my grandmother, Eliza Russell Dawe, had endured. My grandfather, William Dawe, was 20 years older than Eliza and virile at least until his 65th year, when Christina was born – a very pretty, even beautiful child and later a beautiful woman. She always thought of her stern, bearded father as an old man and, with the intuitions of a child, resented his attentions to Eliza. She adored and was her mother's pet, and was indulged as such.

One of those indulgences was a piano; probably the first nod to the arts in that pragmatic family, along with attendance at Bishop Spencer College in St. John's and later Halifax, where she would learn to play it. The piano had been brought in from Bay Roberts and installed in a dark corner of the basement flat off LeMarchant Road, where we lived when I was a child. Although she never went near it otherwise, she would play carols at Christmas and we would sing: "Silent Night," "Away in a Manger" and "O Little Town of Bethlehem" – a word so soft, even in these agnostic, cynical times, it conjures up a sense of peace. She kept a book of carols on the piano, containing the scores and verses of the carols on one page and line-drawing illustrations on the facing page: shepherds and kings, cattle and mangers, candles, bell, wreaths, wise men and a pre-Coca Cola looking St. Nicholas with no Rudolph. I remember it being there summer and winter, a thin green book with heavy lines on thick, pulpy-beige paper, reminiscent of colouring books, perhaps intentionally. Either way, my mother coloured them in with coloured pencils and what I now know were poster paints. I watched her but I was neither encouraged nor invited to participate. I remember the wonder of how her brush strokes especially, but also her penciling, seemed to obey those emphatic lines, sense their authority, and how I admired that. Burned into me is a memory of her colouring a picture of the Virgin and child, the blue robe and the yellow halo. The poster-colour blue still glows like lapis lazuli; the penciled yellow ochre shines like burnished gold. I had crayons and a colouring book of my own, and believed when I was told that "staying inside the line" was the essence of good colouring. That became a factor, and occasionally a burden, in everything I would ever do in my studio and in my life.

Christina and Christopher at Topsail, summer of 1940

2003
Boxing Day

The door to what was once our flat is still there, but boarded up. In the summer of 1943, my parents borrowed some money from my Uncle Lewis Dawe in Bay Roberts and started the construction of a modest house on Waterford Bridge Road. We moved into it on my eighth birthday, December 9, 1943. The house wasn't nearly finished: there were rooms with no wallboard, there was no insulation and no central heating. Although we were looking forward to it, we had to put a lot of effort into having something more than a very bleak Christmas.

That was in the middle, the worst of the war years and one of the many things people on the home front did to help was to fill up drawstring bags known as 'ditty bags' with cigarettes, home-knitted socks, soap, toothpaste, chocolate bars, pocket books, Brylcreem, whatever, to be distributed to people in the active services. You couldn't do that these days because every bag would be suspected of being a bomb. Then, they were simply gifts from home.

My mother filled several such bags. She always put a note in them addressed to the recipient, saying, "If you're ever in St. John's, Newfoundland, we will be living on Waterford Bridge Road, please visit," signed Jack and Christine Pratt.

In those years, gentlemen used to get into their best garb and go calling on Boxing Day. I remember Jimmy Chalker, Ned and Lorne Hiscock, Heber Angel, George Horwood, my uncle Hal Puddester and many others, coming to visit Mom and my Aunty Myrt who lived with us. Dad and Uncle Max Dawe would set out to visit Ev Horwood and Marg Chalker – well, you get the picture.

We were seated with guests at the dinner table, at noon on Boxing Day, when a knock came on the front door. Mom thought it might be an early caller and I was dispatched to let him in. A very young British sailor in uniform, an ordinary seaman, met me at the door. I knew he was an ordinary seaman because we were taught at school to recognize the insignia. He was visibly nervous, even to an eight-year-old. In what must have been a Liverpool, cockney or some other accent I could hardly understand, he asked me if this was the Pratts' house and handed me my mother's note.

I marched him into the dining room, and with childish theatricality announced that we would need another chair. The guests I have referred to were three free-Norwegian naval officers in full uniform: the captain, a man named Johnny Bruenn; the chief engineer known only as "Chieffy"; and the first officer whose name was Biorne. They were off a Corvette doing trans-Atlantic convoy duty – like one of those old WWI boats that Roosevelt lent to Churchill in return for Argentia, etc. As soon as he saw the officers, the ordinary seaman, whose name was Henry, was obviously psyched-out, as we would say nowadays. He didn't know whether to salute or go blind, to make a crude paraphrase. Mom gave him a hug and Aunty Myrt nearly strangled him. As he shook hands all around, my father, Jack, said to him, "I am the skipper on this ship and all below me are of equal rank."

Henry settled in and took a fine tuck aboard, as my aunt would have said. Afterwards we all went into the half-finished living room, where there was a fire in the grate and a Christmas tree in a corner. The air was soon blue with cigar smoke and the hum of brandy. It was like "A Child's Christmas in Wales," which hadn't been written yet, now that I think of it.

Henry paid no attention to the brandy and cigars, but he couldn't take his eyes off the Christmas tree with its shining electric lights. He came over and sat down with me to play with my toys. My mother, who was a sentimental and emotional 'basket case' at the best of times, couldn't handle the sight of this young rating feeling more at home with me than with his naval comrades. Choking back tears, she had to leave the room and have a sip of gin to regain her fragile composure. While callers came and went, Henry and I played Snakes and Ladders and coloured in colouring books all afternoon. Around 5 p.m., when we had finished afternoon tea, he left to rejoin his ship which was docked on the Southside.

The next day, after my father had either gone to work, to bed, or continued calling, Henry unexpectedly showed up at the door with a present for me – a small cylinder of Tinkertoy he had bought at Ayres for around eighty cents. Mom lost it completely again. To put that in perspective, eighty cents could probably have bought four packages of "Gems" or "Flags" in 1943, and Mom figured it might well represent half his week's pay.

Henry and I played with the Tinkertoy all day, making cranes and windmills. Mom gave him some cake and "clingy" before he went back to his ship. His ship was leaving that night in company with Norwegians and Canadians, to join a convoy out of Halifax, bound for Liverpool or Glasgow, or that most fearful destination of them all, around the North Cape and into Murmansk.

As he was leaving, I remember Mom hugging Henry and crying as if he were her own son. He promised to write and about six weeks later we got a letter from him, cleared by the censors, thanking Mom, Dad and Aunt Myrt for their kindness with p.s. – Had Christopher finished building his windmills yet? He promised to send us a card the next Christmas.

The horrors and intensity and ultimate victory of D-Day began before Christmas 1944, and there was no card from Henry, then or ever. For many years after that, sometime during Christmas but usually on Boxing Day, Mom would well up with tears and emotion and say, "I wonder what happened to Henry, he was only a boy."

That was sixty Boxing Days ago. I am sixty-eight and still trying to build windmills.

The house at 93 Waterford Bridge Road, c. 1950

2004

I have seen a lot of old friends lately, people I went to school with; some are widows or widowers, others are divorced. Most of them are retired. What is strange and wonderful is that, in essence, none of them have changed. You meet someone you hadn't spoken to for nearly fifty years and after five minutes, you're not strangers.

Most of them know very little about what artists do, and why should they? Mostly they think of painting as a hobby. "That's how you started," they remind me, and then ask if I am retired now, or soon to be. I used to get on my high horse and say that being an artist is something you are, not just something you do, and therefore the idea of retirement simply isn't part of it. I don't do that anymore.

You feel transparent in the presence of people who knew you when you were very young. Seeing them, the warmth and pleasure of that welcomed familiarity, instructs me that good things do come full circle. So they still think of painting as a hobby, a pastime. I can live with that.

2004

There was a time many years ago, when an active family populated this wonderful house. Now, photographs and phone-calls and an occasional visit serve to remind me of the hundreds of visitors we had, other families joining our own to celebrate the 24th of May, the autumnal equinox or Boxing Day, and the people we visited in return; of evenings spent fishing on the pond, picnics on nearby beaches, outings to 'the Tickles'; of cruising Conception and Trinity Bays on various boats – *Proud Mary, Dry Fly* – confident in the seamanship of our six-person family crew; of our trips to New Brunswick in the Volkswagen bus.

The Salmonier River slips silently along, oblivious to the changes that have happened here or will happen here. The sky has cleared, revealing the beginning of a sunset. The river, curling under the remains of Hurley's Bridge, flows west, merging seamlessly with the waters of St. Mary's Bay, like a life being absorbed into eternity.

2004

I was reading about Matisse last night and learned that he did private things for his own satisfaction, like sculpture for example, which he never sent to market. I suppose it is admitting to some personal want that I never could get excited about Matisse. However, I do envy him his private work, but most of all that it is said that his wife never talked about him, his children never talked about him, his models never talked about him. Two out of three ain't bad.

2004

It is one of those grey-but-bright, soft-shadowed spring mornings. It reminds me of early enthusiasms: enthusiasms for places, activities and adventures that led to *Boat in Sand*, *Two Houses in the Spring*, *Clothesline*, and ten times that number of ideas never realized in actual work. It is a Cape Shore/St. Mary's Bay/Biscay Bay/Cappahayden morning. I am working on two big paintings, and I still have four, large-for-me, primed canvasses (50" x 120", 60" x 70", 50" x 80" and 39" x 89") waiting in the main studio, plus two that are 32" x 84", at a time when I am inclined to work on smaller things. So what to do with them: give some of them away, use them on a one-per-year basis, focus on using them all between now and the retrospective or just leave them where they are for whatever may inspire me? They loom as a challenge and a reminder that the larger things have carried me, as I expected and planned that they would, since the retrospective in 1986. But time, energy, and ambition, and a general dearth of optimism, function differently. Beside me, tacked to the plywood wall, is a handwritten list of sizes of some earlier work: *Cottage* 28" x 45", *Institution* 30" x 30", *Trunk* 36½" x 42'. Successful as they seemed to have been, their small size is no enticement: I believe they would have been much more impressive as images had they been bigger – as I have often observed about the options for my prints, bigger and in paint. I imagine *Institution* 80" x 80," the size of the more narrative subjects I am painting now, or *Cottage* twice its present size at 56" x 90", or *Shop on an Island* 32" x 36" doubled to 64" x 72", not to mention, say,

New Boat, Yacht Wintering, or *Spring at My Place.* Even a current work in progress, *Fall at My Place: The Shadow of Me.* Perhaps it works this way: the more detail there is in an image the smaller it can be; the simpler, the bigger. The minimal works need the authority of scale.

New Boat, Yacht Wintering: neither commemorates the 'flagship' of our early boating years, *Proud Mary,* but that boat now comes to mind, and the time we cruised from Long Pond to Trinity and later to Pope's Harbour, and Deer Harbour on Random Island, where we tied up for the night. I made jiggers for the kids to catch sculpins and connors, just as we used to when I was a boy living in Bay Roberts nearly thirty years earlier. That night Mary fell between the boat and the wharf, and was rescued by Harold Barrett who, with his family, was cruising in company with us aboard their boat *Spindrift.* We sailed to Clarenville the next day where Mary was seen at outpatients and found to have cracked ribs. Despite the discomfort, she stayed aboard for the trip back to Long Pond, which was very rough, especially coming up Conception Bay.

It had also been rough and windy crossing Trinity Bay on our way to Trinity a week earlier, and John, barely sixteen at the time, performed confidently and well on the foredeck to get the jib down. I stayed at the wheel, while Anne attended to the halyard and Barby and Ned took care of the sheets. Mary braved the motion below deck to find dry clothes for John and get supper ready.

That adventure led to other things, as "way leads on to way."

2004

I worked at drawing the *Ferolle Point Light* watercolour until around 3 p.m. yesterday. I got the working drawing transferred onto a sheet of arches aquarelle paper. The transfer now needs to be firmed up before I soak the paper for stretching. I left for Long Pond and the boat around 3:30, but I didn't get much done. Jeanette, who had been in town doing errands all afternoon, met me there and we ate at the club. I went out for a walk after I got home, and after that, I stood for a while on the gravel that, with the water low, is now the riverbank. It was calm and silent and there were smelt schooling in, rippling the surface. I should have been overcome with nostalgia, with memories or longing for times past, but there was none of it. Perhaps nostalgia is actually a problem or a blessing for the young, when memories are fresh enough and sharp enough to rekindle the original emotions. I have to work at it, tell myself I should feel something and ask myself why I do not. Sometimes it is as if the flavours of life beyond yesterday are completely and hopelessly gone.

2004

We drove north past St. Paul's into clear, bright, warming sunlight, to Port au Choix, where I hadn't been for two or three years. We went for a walk along the coast to 'Phillip's Garden' and came back by the trail. It was a spectacular day and a wonderful hike with the added bonus of meeting Pricilla Renouf at the Phillip's Garden dig. She gave us a lot of time and tried to explain what was going on, though I confess that I found it hard to connect the evidence they were uncovering with the thesis she proposed. This is not to question her expertise or accuracy in any way, as it was, no doubt, my own inexperience and ignorance at work. The hike back to the lighthouse parking lot was unimaginably beautiful with the sunlight – sparkling on the Gulf – full in our faces and wildflowers, including dwarf yellow lady's slippers, in bloom on the exposed headland everywhere. I stopped to breathe it in and thought that sometime, perhaps too soon, I will be in some circumstance where I will wish for this, and realized, rhetorically, that this minute is that wish come true.

August 2005
A Painter's Poems

I got a copy of *A Painter's Poems* from Breakwater today. It's a handsome little book, and the self-portrait on the cover ain't bad if I do say so myself. I'm thankful to Clyde Rose and Breakwater for doing it. But it's been a long haul, a long time coming. I had a poem, "How Soon When the Day is White," published in *Atlantic Anthology* that was edited by Will R. Bird back in 1959. It received first prize for poetry in the Arts and Letters competition in 1954. With the exception of one or two poems in books on my work, and a couple of productions featuring readings by Mike Cook, there has been nothing since.

The idea of the book started when we were working on the *Print Catalogue Raisonné* and Clyde saw a few of my poems. He asked me how I felt about submitting a bunch of poems for possible publication, and it went on from there. The first editor he put on my case warned me that if I published my poems without a lot of work – meaning her doctoring 'help' – it could be a humiliation. She not only disliked the way I wrote, but also took exception to what I wrote about. Talk about your non-starter! The second editor assigned shared some of the former's anxieties about the project but was constructive in her approach, and whatever she thought about it, proceeded on the basis that what I write about is my own business. It is happening now because, third time lucky, Clyde has found an editor who seems to have some sympathy, or finds some resonance, in my offerings. Tom Henihan, a soft-spoken and seemingly introspective Irishman, has been in Canada about twenty years or so and, having tried Toronto and the Rocky Mountains, landed in St. John's a year ago. He doesn't want to "go home again to Ireland," but perhaps he likes to be somewhere – if the wind is in the right direction – where he can smell the old sod, or hear echoes of it in the cadences of Water Street.

Either way, we got on very well. He helped me greatly with the initial selection and took a very gentle hand in directing their refinement and presentation. I always felt that he respected the voice, and could relate to the things I write about.

I haven't been prolific: out of a total of ninety-eight poems we wound up with fifty. Writing poetry has always been a way of describing things in a kind of code, things I don't often write about in my diaries. These are always private, closely held matters, that otherwise, perhaps, have no language. I have had input and advice on the merits, dangers and advisability of publishing this work from many sources, and they range from polite encouragement to out-and-out hostility. "It's just a private thing and you should stick with that." "Why risk it – it might be embarrassing." "You should do it so people will see you're really not all that austere." "It's you – why hide it – what have you got to lose?"

Well, we'll see. Tom knows perfectly well that I have no pretensions as a poet and certainly no great expectations for this book. I have the measure of it. It is, I believe, at least honest and deeply felt, and such conscious naiveties as may be present are necessary.

2005

At 5 p.m. in early February, we're driving through the fog, in the wet, musty forest of Terra Nova National Park. The trees are very dark: mixtures of olive green or yellow ochre and ivory black, or burnt sienna with ivory black and perhaps a little purple of some kind in the birches and junipers. In this grey twilight fog, the snow, except where it is stained with road salt and sand, could be said to be colourless. Somehow, there is an atom's thickness, a glaze of pink. Is that because the sun is setting red somewhere behind the overcast, or is it the eye's awareness of its own blood made visible by this neutrality?

Leaving the park, suddenly the trees are sparse and smaller due to incessant harvesting. The fog lifts and we drive toward a brighter sky of pale pearly pinks, oranges and blues, as if the colours of the larger, denser trees in the park were fugitive and leached upward into the fog. Then it is thick again. A swarm of car lights advances toward us, passing each other in a cluster on the three-lane road ahead. They are as I imagine fire-flies to be, or phosphorescence I have seen from creatures swirling in the sailboat's wake. Then they are safely past. I remind Jeanette, who knows but takes the warning in good part, that hydroplaning is a possibility and that in this mild weather moose cannot be trusted not to think it's spring.

2005

Burgeo Road: rough for writing. We drive south to the Annieopsquotch Mountains and eat our lunch at a lay-by there. The snow-glazed hills are capped with mist and shining in the sun. Imbued with an ancestral silence, it is lovely in its way: the sound of the wind in the sparse junipers and alders and distant stands of evergreens, eternal. We guess the mist is local, warmer, moister air, made visible in its rise and passage across the colder hills. It is possible that it could turn seamlessly into a South Coast fog, which might be splendid in itself with sunlight through it and the snow illuminated like the origin of light, but we turn around. It will be Port au Port instead, though it may well be a foggy afternoon there as well. The road is not so much rough as irregular. Jeanette, driving, is silent as I write; she respects my need for privacy, having a need for privacy of her own.

2005

Narrative is most acceptable and sophisticated when it provides a suggestion that something is going on without telling you what it is, when the picture, literally and figuratively, is incomplete, except in its power to imply. It falls down either way if what it tells in total, or suggests in some coy way, is trivial.

2005

Green. The greens – I can't say "green" because, in this rain and with the deciduous trees not yet in leaf, the greens are very rich; dark and heavy in this rain. Mira says green doesn't sell. Blue does. And green seems most acceptable when it is reduced, reddened, compromised into khaki or taupe. Is that because it is the opposite of red – the colour of blood and life? Is the earth less satisfactory and promising than the sky, or its surrogate, the reflecting and transparent sea? Or does green only work in sunlight where, in the distance, it transforms to blue? Or is it because it is so commonplace, so omnipresent? Or a compromise of yellow and blue? What is it about green?

2005

I went for a walk, then after supper decided to go trouting in the pond. It was an ideal evening for it. The sun was full on the trees across the pond and penetrated the woods at its low angle. The colours were wonderful, and the birds, although seeming less numerous than they used to be, 'rang like so many bells.' I got sentimental about the old, dead or dying trees, lit and ennobled by the evening sunlight. They seemed to be fellow travelers, old enough to have presided over and witnessed all our evenings on the pond and all our days and events here at Salmonier. They were peering in the windows of my studio all the years I was drawing from life and the times I put my fist through the silkscreen when I couldn't get the stencil right. They have seen things fly through the glass: squeegees, hammers and – once – a chair.

I remembered one evening when I was in my teens, looking at some tall, healthy trees up the river at Uncle Cal's place, where Bernadette and Dick live now. I was there with Dad and his cousin Ewart. That was near the end of my grandfather's life, and I was thinking that those trees would outlive him, that their relative anonymity made them eternal anyway. I am the age now that he was then.

Although the pond seemed dead, I did catch four small trout. The first and largest one I kept but I felt bad about killing it, so I shook the other three off the end of the hook. A nostalgic, heritage meal of sea-run trout and brewis would be ok, but there are many things I would rather eat than pond trout. That death was unnecessary. In the end, the best and most rewarding part of the evening was the row in the old boat.

2005

Wild Cove, 18 degrees Celsius and a very low tide. The smell of exposed seabed and seaweed carries rich in the warm, humid air. Mrs. West used to get romantic about the smell of the sea expressed in the landwash. Mr. West used to say "clam flats," dismissively. I always felt greatly out of place in their home, but never unwelcome. I didn't like the claustrophobia of Fredericton, if that's what it was. I did feel inferior, the causes and reasons were many and inadvertent. Mr. West believed that there should be learning in a house: art, music, literature, none of which had been priorities in our home. He had found the seeds of that in his home at Coles' Island and believed it should be a major component of a more sophisticated life in Fredericton. He was well read and very intelligent but, on a deeper level, none of that meant anything to him. He considered the ability to shoe a horse, feed your family on a farm, drive logs on a river, run a sawmill or a shop, far more important in the measure of a man than anything he had learned at Harvard. It was that part of him I liked and admired. He always treated me with kindness and respect and I had great respect for his war service, his sense of civic responsibility, and the integrity he brought to the high offices he held.

He often used analogies that recalled his life on the farm and in the logging operations. He said to me once that my father looked like "a bull that had been hit over the head by a maul." I was hurt by that, but later I was encouraged to believe what he meant was that, somewhere along the line, my father had been dealt a 'bad hand.' Of course, that is what I wanted and still want to believe, but I have found it difficult, and it has always got in the way.

2005

There are photographs of my father, when he was about twenty-six years old, wearing a suede leather windbreaker. I remember it from Topsail, where we rented rooms in a farmhouse for the summer months from 1939 to 1943. I was seven then and he was thirty-three. It was heavy, stained and matted, with stretched, bulging pockets, smelling dark and organic. I remember how heavy it felt, laid on the shoulders of a child – to "make a man of him."

I dreamt about my father last night. He was alive and visiting Newfoundland but didn't seem interested in getting in touch with any of us. Probably by accident, he had come into contact with Mary, who was some reincarnation of my mother, who he didn't know was dead. I caught a glimpse of him: he was about fifty, the occasional drinking was over and he looked healthy and quietly content. He was wearing the suede jacket, which looked crisp and new.

Jack Pratt at Witless Bay, c. 1935

He obviously had a new life that seemed to be in Australia or New Zealand where he had a small farm that, along with his savings from his former life, kept him modestly comfortable. Like a man falsely accused who has served his time, distrustful of the world he had gone elsewhere to live with a few new loyal acquaintances who did not mistake compassion for naiveté, or generosity for wealth. It was sad, but I was happy for him.

I have had that dream in various settings many times since he died, and 'crisp and new' is how I would imagine the jacket if I did not remember it, but I do.

2005

The railway car in *Jack's Dream of Summer* could be anywhere, and I want anyone who looks at it to be able to locate it in his or her own imagination. It has only a horizon to tell you it is by an immense lake or the sea – that is infinity. But in my imagination, as I was painting it, it was located near the Flambro Cliffs on a headland north of Ochre Pit Cove, where you can sense the curvature of the earth and 'see forever' as they say. I go there frequently for that sense of the infinite. I don't think Jack, my father, ever did. His infinities were elsewhere.

Chester Dawe and Jack Pratt aboard Hemmer Jane, Labrador, 1971

2005
Reunion

The PWC Class of '52 reunion reception went very well, diminished only by the absence of many people who were there last time, but upbeat regardless. Jeanette was very warmly received and accepted. Everybody seems to be happy for us, which means a lot to me especially, since I am the old comrade. The evidence of the exponential march of time was everywhere.

We went to Bay Bulls for a boat cruise and dinner theatre on Saturday night. Following the clearing that came on Friday, the last day of the midsummer month dawned clear, sunny and warm, allowing for a very pleasant hour whale watching before the dinner theatre. The crowd from away were no more excited than those of us who have stayed at home, and Harold and Jean Schwartz from Deer Lake got more excited than most. Jeanette and I were last into the restaurant and sat with Sonia at the only place left – a three-person table at the back of the room. Perhaps that was appropriate, despite the warmth and camaraderie of the event. Sonia and I are cousins, and have always been slightly peripheral to the main stream of things, and closer to eachother than to anyone external, but that is overly analytical and unnecessary to say after a perfect day. For Jeanette and me, driving home across the Witless Bay Line with the stars bright in the dark summer sky was close to being the best of it.

We had a picnic at Murray's Pond at noon today. The picnic was perfect in its way: warm weather, sunshine and friendship, no drugs, nobody drunk, nothing more than fundamentally good people concerned about and liking one another and very happy to be together. Who knows, perhaps that's it forever? Every day, from one quarter or another, there is news of someone, either close or well known to us, who is stricken. It is no longer morbid to wonder who is next on the list, a list that none of us wants to see but must acknowledge.

2005

I left Salmonier alone at 10:30 a.m., Jeanette having gone to Point La Haye to spend Christmas Day with her mother. There was a clear blue sky, no wind, and it was mild and dry. No day could ever embody the idea of 'peace on earth' more than this. I drove across a snow-paved Southeast River Road, taking photographs along the way. At the Two Mile Falls on the Southeast River, I did a mini-essay of photographs in circumstances that were as close as they can ever be to spiritual for me. And, in my imagination, deep in the sparkle and effervescence where that golden-brown water tumbled and roared over the rocks, there were ghosts of giant flawless salmon emerging and vanishing again into its turbulence – fish wise enough to know the dangers of summer, going to their ancient spawning channels under the benign cover of winter. As always, I stopped to pay my respects at the burned cabin site.

At Pt. Verde in the early afternoon, I finished my Christmas dinner: some potato salad Jeanette made and a ham and turkey sandwich I made myself. I washed it down with hot, strong tea and had two squares of dark, bitter chocolate for desert. I had the wagon door ajar and could hear the sea, calm except for windlines breathing on the beach and the occasional gull complaining. It would have been less silent without these sounds: they made the silence palpable, tolerable, providing evidence that this was not the silence of death, but a gift to the living. It was entirely peaceful. I went for a walk along the beach.

I had a good walk at Pt. Verde, clean and serene. At 3 p.m. I pulled over on a loop of the old road on a hill just north of Red Head River, overlooking St. Mary's Bay. I could see Salmonier Arm beyond Little Colinet Island and the whole length of Great Colinet Island further south. Point La Haye is directly across the bay: had it been an hour later, Jeanette could have seen my headlights flashing across that distance. I drank the last of the tea that by then had taken on a more emphasized thermos taste. I finished my dark, bitter chocolate and a pot of yogurt and tidied up before getting back on the pavement to complete the loop. There was no wind, yet the land, the wilderness, seemed to have an inaudible roar. I have never had a more satisfactory Christmas.

2006

The power of this place is not in its mountain grandeur. It is in the way the air moves across the land, even when it is blowing hard. It is often too subtle to describe simply as wind: it is a chill – as a ghost is said to chill – or a breath, a whisper, always seductive, potentially sinister. It seems to be something exhaled by the hills themselves.

I don't know what it is. I just feel it every time I am here: it tells me I am a visitor, transitory, unimportant. I don't know what it is.

2006

The weather stayed fine yesterday, so we had a good morning here with the doors and windows open and a breeze blowing through. I did get some meaningful work done on the watercolours before we left for Bay Roberts for the afternoon and on to the Brigus Blueberry Festival for the evening.

Barby, Philip Jr. and Peter met us at Bay Roberts where we had a nice afternoon. I – meaning my hip – felt pretty grungy when we got there, but I went for a walk anyway. Around the garden first, then out to Watering Cove and down the steps to Lower Cove Beach, which I had to climb later, followed by a brisk walk back to the cabin. I felt much better for it afterwards. Peter cut his heel on a mussel shell and left a goodly drop of his DNA at Lower Cove. Barby had a good first aid kit in her car, and while she went to get it, Jeanette administered a cold, sea water cloth to stanch the bleeding. It all turned out ok. Meanwhile, Ned, Jacob and Claire arrived at the cabin and joined us at Lower Cove. In a fleet of three vehicles, we arrived at Brigus on schedule at 6:00.

The weather was perfect for the fireworks and the BBQs and the food as good as it always is at brother Philip's. I don't know what we would have done or, more specifically, what I would have done without Philip and Kitty and the sanctuary their home in Brigus has provided me for the past several years. The Farmers, the Staveleys and Anne Budgell were there in addition to family. The kids, all except the pleasantly sophisticated Claire, scrambled down over the cliff and played on the rocks. They ate only hotdogs, and until the fireworks started, kept themselves occupied, fixated on a 'game of cubes,' or whatever they are called. The fireworks couldn't be described as spectacular, but as good as it gets for an unpretentious local event. Watching the lights come up in Brigus as the sun set over the timeless profile of the hills was the best of it.

So I'll get back at it today, do a bit more with the watercolours, and, optimistically, maybe order stretcher bars for a soon-to-be oil painting or two.

2006

I realized while we were driving through Parsons Pond, Portland Creek, River of Ponds – all the way north – that my memories of the times I came here with my father and Fred Clarke and Philip are fading. Those memories are becoming very distant, giving way to more recent associations born of my own travels here with Jeanette. That is true of further north also, mostly because Jeanette and I have gone so many places, hiked and done so many things with focus and intensity. I do remember the very poignant moments: the drive from Roddickton to St. Anthony alone with Dad, the picnic with David Silcox and Fred Clarke just north of Belburns, and the days I spent sketching on Portland Creek sands while Dad and the others went fishing on *Brian's Feeder*, but that's about it. I have to dig for the rest as I do for the one time I went as far as Point Riche with Mary; and my hippy summer in the VW bus, 1971, now seems like another lifetime to me. There is sunlight on Gros Morne Mountain. I still have an absurd fading dream of climbing it.

2007

On a calm, pleasantly cool early afternoon in May, we went walking at Western Brook. The brook was in spate but still 'clear as gin.' For an hour and a half we ambled on the sands, piled up deep to landward and strewn with driftwood and litter, the result of a 'hundred year' storm and tide last fall or winter. We then drove ten minutes north to St. Paul's, to an accustomed lay-by on a coastline loop of the old road where we had our lunch of tea, bagels with light cream cheese and jam from home.

At 4:00 p.m., we stopped again at Squid Cove for a 'mug-up' of thermos tea, with crackers and 'hard cheese' from Steady Brook. It was strange to see 'longers' laid out on the ground with the usual neat piles of lobster pots absent for their season at sea, and smoke coming from the chimneys of the lobster camps while the boats hauled their traps a few hundred feet offshore. A brief season of excitement, of hard, get-it-while-you-can work balanced with cabin living. A brief season of camaraderie tempered by rivalry, the nostalgia of cooking on a small woodstove and sex in a narrow bunk, of remembering how it used to be through the rose windows of how it is. A very brief season.

2007

Jeanette and I hiked from Cape Norman out to Whale Point and around to Wild Cove, then followed the old road back. We spent half an hour on the rough, flat, gently sloping, concrete-like rocks at the northernmost tip of the point. There was no seaway to speak of, nothing more than the beginnings of a wind-lop sloshing around and occasionally 'surging' into the lowest tide pools. However, it was evident by the extent of the naked, water-worn limestone that Whale Point can be a fearsome, spectacular place. It is well named: we saw several very active humpbacks feeding close inshore. All that under a clear blue sky in a cool freshening breeze made it an entirely satisfactory afternoon, and with all due respect to Crouse, gave us cause to regret not having spent the whole day at Pistolet Bay.

2007

It is 28 degrees Celsius and the height of summer here at Salmonier. I pack a small lunch before leaving to make another nostalgia trip, a memorial round of Southeast Placentia and the Cape Shore. I will brave the rough, dirt road – that is part of it – and risk the disillusionment of visiting the Beaver Falls alone.

The drive across the Southeast River road is rough and dusty as usual at this time of year. It is a hard road, a skin of gravel scraped across a bed of trampled rock. I make my pilgrimage to the Beaver Falls and discover the steps leading down have disappeared and the concrete retaining wall has fallen in, leaving jagged spikes of rebar sticking out to trip and tear. This makes the descent dangerous but, ironically, provides useful handholds on the way up. It is a place full of memories for me, summed up by reference to the roar and sparkle of the falls and the smell of the peat-brown water. If any place may be construed to be a 'holy place,' then this is a holy place, a place of spirits, for me. I try to converse with them but, like music, the language of the water needs no words. I say a prayer and, like Thomas, ask for a sign. I don't think this is unreasonable, after all we have been encouraged and instructed to believe. But there is no sign: we ask and a seemingly indifferent God tells us to go to hell.

I stopped at the remains of the cabin and now I am at Pt. Verde. It is bright, breezy and very warm with only an occasional crow interrupting the sound of the sea. I decide to go for a walk. The beach bears witness to huge waves and violent storms but there is no evidence of caplin on this once fecund shore, no stranded dogfish or cod, only one lumpfish with a crater for an eye. A seal, which at first shines like a black glass float, silently dissolves into the sea to protest my presence, but the terns are strident and vocal in their displeasure.

Branch Country is very green. Two male loons are fighting; one chases the other while the female looks on. Although they can fly, the fighting loons, using their wings as oars, bat their way across the pond. During a short truce, all three settle in a group until it begins again and the chased bird is banished to a corner of the arena. After a breather, he takes off, flying low over the couple as he passes them, then climbs, his species' classic call seeming to mock his adversary as he disappears over the surrounding hills.

There were no salmon to be seen, either in the Beaver Falls or at the Two Mile on the Southeast. I didn't expect there would be, any more than I expected a 'sign,' so I'm not disappointed. It has been a good day.

2007

L'anse aux Meadows on a cool, windy, overcast morning. There are traces of snow on the tops of the Sacred Islands and some on the hills above Cape Onion, visible in the near distance to the west. Parked at the end of the road in L'anse aux Meadows village, I can see the loom of Belle Isle to the north, a pale grey shape you wouldn't notice if you didn't know it was there. The summer people are gone and the Viking realities and pretensions alike have been abandoned for the realities of winter in this eternal landscape. Neat sticks of greenish pressure-treated lumber attend the preparations for off-season make-work projects: trails, boardwalks, picnic tables, platforms and heritage lookouts. I now understand what people mean when they say that in the absence of a viable resource-based economy, catering to tourists – building trails, tables and toilets for their comfort – is ultimately demeaning.

2007

At Quirpon on this ninth day of March, there is just a draught of wind but it feels much colder than -6°C. There is something intoxicating, sweet and satisfactory about this cold air. It is the raw, open, geophysical cold of the true north, not the Arctic, to be sure, though the sea is white with pack ice borne on the Labrador Current to all horizons. Does cold air, like cold water, hold and release more oxygen than when it is warm? The body and the spirit seem to welcome, even to relish it, but the cynic observes, only in small, safe doses with warmth and shelter nearby.

At L'anse aux Meadows, Jeanette and I park at a great spot for lunch with warm full sunlight filling the wagon from the south. Directly ahead to the northeast is Quirpon Island and Cape Bauld. To the north, Little Sacred Island and to the northeast Great Sacred Island. Just to the right of Little Sacred Island, we can see the pale, smoky loom of Belle Isle itself, its distant grandeur is hard to describe, too faint to photograph. There are common eiders and scoters feeding in the open leads between the icepans close inshore, and a raven croaking somewhere.

Lunch is a toasted multigrain bagel with light cream cheese and homemade partridgeberry jam, yogurt and tea from Tuckamore for a chaser. Reader, sometime, somewhere hence, know this: it doesn't get any better than this for Christopher Pratt.

Cape Onion and the Sacred Islands

May 2007
Retrospective

We had a smooth flight home from Québec City yesterday with no delays. Even our baggage was off the plane early and intact. No matter where I travel, arriving back in Newfoundland, landing in Torbay, is always like stepping ashore. This journey began in Ottawa with the opening of the retrospective of my work at the National Gallery of Canada in September 2005. The show is now hanging at its final venue at the Musée national des beaux-arts du Québec. It was a good experience from the start to finish, with the last leg of the journey being every bit as positive as the beginning.

The media preview in Ottawa went reasonably well. Some of the interviews got a bit heavy and I was quite fatigued. I was aware I was repeating myself towards the end. We went to a neighbourhood lunch stop with Josée Drouin-Brisebois afterwards, then headed back to the gallery to sign a few books and spend some time with the conservation people. *The Island* and *Gulf of St. Lawrence*, both in the same collection, were in really bad shape. We didn't reach any conclusions, but the preliminary consensus was that exposure to light and possibly careless cleaning were factors. None of the other paintings hanging seemed to have similar problems, except *In the Heat of Summer*, which had some areas that looked like 'blooming.'

We had time for a bit of a rest before going to David Marshall's home for dinner, where we had East Indian food at a beautifully appointed table. He was an entirely gracious host and the other guests were exceedingly pleasant. David's patronage has made this retrospective possible.

On the morning of the opening there was a reception for the staff that was well attended. Barby, with Philip Jr. and Peter, plus Christopher and Keir, arrived in time after a bumpy flight. Katherine and Elizabeth got in by bus. Ned and Gabrielle, John and Tracey, Philip and Kitty and cousin Janet were already on the ground and Anne was in Ottawa on business, so it was almost a full crew aboard.

It is not an exaggeration to say that I was overwhelmed by the installation at the National Gallery and by the air of celebration that surrounded me at the opening itself. The logic and insight of Josée Drouin-Brisebois' selection of works, and the space afforded them, brought dignity and clarity to the show. Pierre Théberge's remarks were complimentary without being disproportionate to the work or the occasion. He left the impression that he was totally supportive of the project.

The dinner following the opening went very well: Jeanette and I were seated with Pierre, Mira, Philip and Kitty, David Silcox and Linda Intaschi and Senator Serge Joyal. John, Anne, Barby and Ned sat at different tables. I thought afterwards that David, Philip and I should have had a toast to absent comrades – Dad, Bob, Fred and Uncle Chester – late of the *Hemmer Jane*.

∾

We were late getting to Halifax because of a raging storm, so we missed a luncheon Jeff Spalding had organized, where I was scheduled to give a talk on my work. That went ahead anyway, with Josée standing in for me, following what I am told was a gallant and generous introduction to the topic by Alex Colville. Madame Myra Freeman, Lieutenant Governor of Nova Scotia, opened the show the following night. She was eloquent and gracious in her remarks. There were a lot of people there, many of them old friends I hadn't seen for a very long time. I spoke about that, thanked Ray Cronan for the installation and his attention to detail, and Jeff for his input into the show from its inception.

We had breakfast with Josée the next morning and went to a party at Dawn McNutt's in the evening. Most of the people there were Mt. A class of '56 or '57: Nancy Ellis Stevens, Graham and Kay Frampton, Merle Pratt, Jim Wells, Tom, Will, and Monica Forrestall – so a lot of the chat was prefaced by "remember when." The Forrestalls had to leave early – our classmate Natalie Forrestall was gravely ill. Seeing Tom, talking shop and chatting about old times in company with Dawn, Nancy … was the high point of Halifax for me.

Caroline Stone's installation of the show at The Rooms in St. John's was well spaced and sensitively lit. At the opening, the Hon. Ed Roberts, Lieutenant Governor of Newfoundland and Labrador and, like me, a graduate of Prince of Wales, was articulate and generous in his introduction. His father, Dr. Harry Roberts, was a high school classmate of my father's at the Methodist College. When he referred to our parents' friendship, I remembered how I had started painting while convalescing after his father had removed my appendix in 1952. When I got up to say a few words, the reality of having my life's work showing in that amazing building, whose principal architect was my brother Philip, and the presence of friends and relatives, people who had known me for seventy years, the emotion of the occasion took over and my speech sputtered out not long after I got into it. Mary wasn't there. Perhaps she felt that would make things easier for both of us, but it remained difficult, and nonetheless emotional for me to express the full measure of appreciation I have for her solidarity and warmth in the early years. From the windows of The Rooms, I could see the hospital where I was born, all the places I had lived, gone to school and church, and the cemetery where my parents, grandparents and great-grandparents are buried. My mind turned to them and I wondered what they would think about it all: would they be proud, and would that pride be tempered by a suspicion of excess?

❧

In Winnipeg, Mary Jo Hughes, who was in charge of the retrospective at that venue, met us at the airport and delivered us to the Fairmont. After we got settled in, Anne called and we had supper with her at the hotel that evening. She seemed well and happy. There was a lot of talk of 'home': Barby and Ned, their circumstances and life at Salmonier. After dessert, Jeanette excused herself so we could have father-daughter privacy for an hour. Seeing Anne and talking with her was a welcome and timely reminder of the things I sometimes forget in her absence. The following evening, we walked around the corner for dinner at the director's digs – a nicely furnished loft in an old factory or warehousing building. Also on hand that evening were Mary Jo, Pierre Aucin and his partner Tom, Mayo Graham of the National Gallery of Canada, and Gordon Gage, Chair of the Winnipeg Gallery's Board. It was a nice evening with good food and the chat didn't get arty or heavy, which is always a big plus.

The day before the opening, we spent most of the time at the gallery. I learned that Josée was in town and that she would have some input into hanging the show. I did press interviews until noon with CTV, Shaw and the *Winnipeg Free Press*. I was my usual gabby self; all of it seeming rehearsed after fielding the same questions for many years.

On the day of the opening, we had lunch with Mary Jo at the gallery restaurant and spent a couple of hours at 'the show' observing and making notes. Again, the hanging and presentation were superb. Having spent most of the day at the gallery, we went back to the hotel to rest before meeting Josée for supper at the Delta, en route to the opening. There was a good turnout and it was a real plus for me that Anne was there. The speeches were short and crisp, including my own, and I spent the next couple of hours talking to people directly about my work. The highlight of the evening was meeting my late cousin Irene's children – Shelagh, Jim and Tracey. I didn't know they existed and I think they were surprised that I connected with who they were. They didn't know much about their Dawe origins but were very interested. I told them I would send them 'stuff', and, of course, I introduced them to Anne.

The article in the *Winnipeg Free Press* was sensitive and positive. I got nervous when its author, Morley Walker, called one morning to ask me a few personal questions. I didn't refuse to comment, but I was careful. He handled it very well and got Jeanette – at "forty something" – into the piece, succinctly describing the new reality.

∽

In Québec City, I was again a stranger. From our twentieth story hotel room, we could look down on the whole topography of the Plains of Abraham. Upriver, we could see the route I took sailing through here in 1974, 1977 and 1983, and the marina where we tied up and provisioned before heading out into the Gulf of St. Lawrence.

The opening at the Musée national des beaux-arts du Québec went well with lots of people and a warm and courteous response. I was, of course, worried about the potential language barrier, but people were very patient with me. It was all very special, including the press reception earlier in the day. So the final venue of the show began on a very good and satisfactory note.

After the opening, we had a fine time at a restaurant in old Québec with Lien Quillet, Québec curator of the show, Josée, Mishiko Gagnon and Monica Gagnon, Mssrs. Michel Martin and John Porter, Musée Director, who wore a red sports jacket that would have looked well on the often natty Uncle Chester! Ninety percent of the conversation was in English as a courtesy to Jeanette and me. That totally belies the reputation many would assign to a major Québec institution.

Before we left Québec City, I visited the show alone. By previous agreement, twenty of the works had been returned to their owners earlier in the tour, but the remaining work was hung with understanding and respect, as it had been everywhere. I made notes in the small Moleskine notebook Josée had given me on my sixty-ninth birthday, as I had at the National Gallery and at Winnipeg and twenty-one years earlier, when the 1985 Vancouver retrospective was in St. John's, and later at the Art Gallery of Ontario. The bottom line is that I want to keep my eye on the prize: to savour and celebrate my existence, and to guard and maintain whatever quality I am capable of bringing to my work. Through this retrospective, as in 1985, I have had the opportunity to determine what is strong and what is weak, what is worthwhile and what is a waste of time in my work. Occasionally the lines are blurred; there are few absolutes. But I do know, if only after the fact, when I let the side down, and it is usually through the "ah boy, what the hell – that's good enough – who's going to notice anyway" process that it happens.

Québec City has been the last opening of what will almost certainly be the last retrospective in my lifetime and it has gone well. But things are different now from what they were in 1985. I was 50 then – it was mid-career or so – and I could reasonably have a twenty-year plan. At seventy-one, a twenty-year plan seems overly optimistic. The danger is of thinking of it as a 'wrap,' but I will not.

Here at Salmonier, there were two geese with five very small goslings feeding on the lawn at dawn this morning. As we left the gallery yesterday to go to dinner, there were skeins and vees of snow geese flying north, high overhead. John Porter told us the geese would have stopped over at Lac St. Pierre, upriver of Trois Rivieres, the body of water where, with a sharp northeasterly blowing against the current at the running out, we encountered the steepest chop to greet us on our way home in *Proud Mary* in 1974. It comes around: two retrospectives later, who would have thought ... and why?

Jeanette and Christopher Pratt, Notre Dame Bay, 2007

2007
Class Picnic

Perfect weather and good attendance for the class picnic at Joanne and David Templeton's in Upper Gullies yesterday. I had a good chat with Roland Thornhill, which I had decided to do in case there had been any misunderstandings following our earlier 'give and take' banter. Of course, there were none. The fear on my part that there might have been was unfair to him. He told me how, after winning a national public speaking award when we were in grade 11 at Prince of Wales, our homeroom teacher, Ray Curnew, had taken him aside and instead of the customary "Thornhill," said, simply, "I'm proud of you, Roland." I remembered how Ray had spoken to me after a debate on the Memorial Stadium issue, where I had defended the proposition that the Provincial Government should put money into that St. John's project in 1952. We debaters were sent out to wait in the hall while the class voted to decide the winner. I lost, but Ray found an opportunity after the event and told me, "You lost the popularity contest, Pratt, but in my opinion you won the debate." It gave me an insight into myself: I would have preferred the former. He told me not to be afraid to have ambition. Ray Curnew was an extraordinary man. We were all privileged to have him as a teacher and the many, superficially comic tales about him, attest to his presence and influence.

I was stiff, tired, sun-baked, overfed and dehydrated by the time we got home. It had started to rain. We decided to have a rest in the studio with the rain pecking and plopping on the skylight. It had been quite the weekend, and it was good to see how old friendships quickly dissolve the space between their last encounters.

Now there is the reality of ongoing work waiting in the studio. Not assuming that they care, but nonetheless, not wanting to let my classmates down, I will get back to it. If that sounds like rhetorical blather, Dear Diary, it is not. To read it as such – as Cyril Poole once admonished me when I questioned the sincerity of his, Otto Tucker's and others' singing of old Methodist hymns at a house party following a function at Grenfell College – "Would be totally to misunderstand."

2007

We are driving on a dry road, bordered by junipers and the fall colours of the barrens, under a blue sky with two levels of scattered clouds. CBC weather says it is raining on the West Coast, but there is, as always, an optimism in the sunshine casting a shadow of my hand across this page. Jeanette and I are met with the acrid stench of Arnold's Cove refinery and, as the politicians follow Smallwood's dream of turning Placentia Bay into "Sudbury by the Sea," the prospect for more to come. But I am easily transported to another time, of my own youth in Newfoundland, and tales heard told. I can still imagine walking across the barrens with the brooks and gullies full of red-bellied mud trout and coveys of partridge exploding from the 'tucks' ahead of me.

Local outdoor columnists now refer to mud trout as 'brookies,' a term picked up from American outdoor sportsmen's magazines. 'Brookies', 'bunnys': why do they apply terms of endearment to creatures they intend to kill? What imagined status does that imply? I remember when I was ten years old, catching a richly coloured mud trout in the Southeast River at a time of year when its anadromous brethren, in bright silver livery, were returning to the river from the sea. Showing it to my father, I announced grandly that I had caught "a great eastern brook trout" – a term I had gleaned from either *Field and Stream* or *Outdoors*, both of which I bought regularly at the time. My father looked at me with a toss of his head that indicated bemused annoyance and said, "Is that so now, Christopher? Looks like a mud trout to me."

Jeanette and I went for a walk up the Nine Mile Road this morning and on our way back, Jim Power, who was driving down Walsh's Hill from visiting friends, stopped to say hello. Not a feather out of him. We talked about the recent heavy rain, flooding, global warming, the continuing decline of salmon stocks in the river, and bakeapples. Jim was hoping Jeanette's brother Dominic, over in Trepassey, could get him another gallon or two. We came home, had a snack, and then left to do our monthly drive around the Cape Shore, back via Branch and the Western Shore, and hike at Cape St. Mary's on the way.

It was a beautiful afternoon there, hot and cold, with the thousands of black and white gannets echoing that contrast against an imperially blue sea and sky. Back at the wagon on the interpretation centre parking lot, we got out the yogurt and muffins and poured ourselves mugs of thermos tea. I called home to get my messages, but the cell phone reception was faint and broken. There was one message: Brenda had called asking me to call her when I could and that was it. But I have known Brenda since she was a child and there was no mistaking the distress in her voice. So we decided to head back up the Cape Shore to a place where I knew the reception would be better. I also knew that if anyone in my family was in trouble and neither I nor Jeanette could be reached, the first person anyone would call would be Brenda.

I parked at Pt. Verde, at the same spot I have always parked since the days we had the cabin on the Southeast. I got out of the wagon, wandered on that grass and crowberry hummock, and made the call. Brenda answered right away. I said, "Hi – you wanted me to call." She said, "Christopher ... Dad died at two o'clock this afternoon." She gave me some particulars, and I told her how we had seen her father just hours before that, and how well and animated Jim had been. I felt very sad for Brenda, her self-discipline and intelligence always in control of an inner fragility. I also felt sad for her siblings: Sandra, Elaine, David, Brian and Susan, and especially for their mother – the strong, caring, intelligent, dignified Elsie who had, so suddenly and unexpectedly, lost her husband of over fifty years. Jim Power, and two years ago, Tom Walsh, both of them my age – decent, hard working, no nonsense men, friends and neighbours for forty-five years, gone.

I forgave myself the immense relief I felt when I knew it wasn't one of my own. Jeanette, waiting in the wagon, said she had known that from the look on my face.

"It is the plight that man was born for.
It is Margaret you mourn for."
    Gerard Manley Hopkins: "Margaret, are you grieving ..."

Brenda and Elsie

August 2007
Jersusalem

We had intended to work today, but it was a warm, very beautiful morning and life is short. I ask myself: What are the odds of any individual human consciousness ever seeing the light? And speculate: one to the square of the sum total of all the atoms in the universe, and figure that may be conservative. So we decided to go over to Western Bay for a walk.

We walked out to the beacon on Western Bay Head, then south along the coast by the old, fallen fence of what was once a community pasture, a 'common,' to the long-abandoned Bradley's Cove. I wondered if my great-grandfather, the Rev. John Pratt, visited there often when he was the Methodist preacher at Western Bay. It dawned on me that he would have blessed or scolded my grandfather Jim and his younger brother Ned in a Yorkshire accent. We climbed the cleared land that was once pasture and potato ground, and sat close together eating perfect blueberries by the fistfull, and watched gulls and ravens riding uplift at the edge of Rose's Cliffs. How strange to be looking down at soaring birds.

We got to the old Bradley's Cove road where it leaves Adam's Cove, and followed it back toward Western Bay. There were sheep everywhere on the hills, sheltering by the ruins and in the old cellars. I caught myself humming the Parry setting of Blake's Jerusalem and thought to myself: "And did those feet in ancient times ..." I do that often; but not in respect of the Reverend John, who already believed in God. Jeanette is 30 – well, 29¼ years younger than me; she knows what's going on.

September 2007
Cape Onion/Cape St. Mary's

After hiking at Cape Onion for an hour and a half, we had a cup of tea with David and Barbara Adams at their 'Tickle Inn' before leaving on the long drive down the coast to Corner Brook. We drove west to Eddies Cove East, then through Green Island Brook, Savage Cove, Deadman's Cove, Anchor Point ... and south along the Straits to Eddies Cove West. Further south, past Squid Cove, Port au Choix, River of Ponds ... we stopped at Old House Rocks and Western Brook to wander around, so it was midnight by the time we checked in at the Glynmill Inn.

The ride home from Corner Brook yesterday was good; humming along, roof open, through warm, breeze-buffeting sunlight with not much traffic. We stopped at Grand Falls for lunch, and took a side trip to the Salmonid Centre. There has been a good run of salmon this year, but the few late comers waiting to move upstream from the viewing tank looked more like kelts than the bright fish we saw heading upstream to spawn earlier. There was the usual moose-eyed fog between Arnold's Cove and the Whitbourne turn off.

Back in Salmonier, I want – as always – to affect a seamless transition from that roaming, collecting, endless-day life into my studio experience. I want it to be as easy as stepping from a boat onto a wharf when the tide is high. But there is mail waiting on the table, the phone is ringing, the fax machine is licking out its type-faced tongue at me, and the lawn needs mowing. The Salmonier River slips into St. Mary's Bay as oblivious to our comings and goings as I am mindful, after forty-five years living here, of its regular, metronomic moon-driven ins and outs. The wind is from the west and there isn't a cloud in the sky, so I decide I need to ease back into it. We pack our standard lunch and head for Cape St. Mary's, stopping at the usual stations of that ritual along the way: Rocky River, Beaver Falls, Pt. Verde, Goosberry Cove ... returning home from Gannet Rock via Branch country, Red Head River, Harricott...

Cape Onion to Cape St. Mary's: an 1100-km drive across this ever-amazing Island.

I'll get back to work tomorrow.

Jeanette at Cape St. Mary's, August 2007

EPILOGUE

WHEN I go into the art supply store, I remember how the very sight of tubes of Winsor & Newton watercolours used to excite me, how nature excited me. It would be nice to feel that artless, unselfconscious enthusiasm again, to be able to work indifferent to my own precedents and without concern for expectations people may have about my work. Just to be in love with light, and wind, and water lapping on the shore, the sense of wilderness, the sense of home.

My mother and father at Bay Roberts, c. 1934

Self-Portrait: Who is this Sir Munnings?, 1998, mixed media,
Collection RBC Financial Group

ABOUT THE COVER

I WAS looking for a more contemporary photograph of myself
to incorporate into one of the small collages I was working on
and I came across a snapshot from 1996 that was, it seemed to me,
saturated with "attitude" and "arrogance" and reminded me of an
anecdote I had read about Picasso:

Sir Alfred Munnings was, for a time, President of the Royal British
Academy, and during his tenure had taken some ill-advised
and stupid potshots at the rapidly ascending Picasso. Picasso,
ever sensitive to criticism and slight from whatever menial or
inconsequential source, even at the peak of his fame and powers,
on hearing about this particular incident, had asked, perplexed,
"Who is this Sir Munnings?" I was struck by the power of
that probably inadvertent putdown, this almost peasant
contemptuousness: the British would say "Sir Alfred," not "Sir
Munnings," and it would have to be Lord Munnings; a small

matter perhaps, but it resonated, and remembering things like honourary doctorates and my Order of Canada (a photocopy of the badge is collaged onto the portrait), my response to that photograph of me was, "Who is *this* Sir Munnings?"

I had been working on a painting before the fire, called *Above Cabot Street*. It survived without damage, but it was going nowhere. I lived above Cabot Street until I was seven years old and have vivid memories of that, so it was already an autobiographical image. I painted out everything except the iron fence and background trees and bushes in preparation and then photocopied the snapshot on tissue paper to be stuck in place. The photocopier I used is ancient and yielded a very rough and ready product on several sheets which had then to be joined — I thought of having a more sophisticated enlargement made in St. John's, but mine seemed more in character with a deliberately self-deprecating "take." Other traces, ghosts, of *Above Cabot Street* are visible, especially the end of a retaining wall, adjacent to the left arm.

I also added some photocopies of myself at various ages and stages at the bottom of the work, together with those of a girl I knew and cared about when I was fourteen. She was twenty-six when she died, in 1963; the photo I worked from was sent to me by a mutual friend. I found the quotation in Dylan Thomas — at random, believe it or not: I closed my eyes and stuck my finger in a book of his collected poems and there it was. I could not have found anything more apt. The collage is about her as well, and I have since used the photograph in other collages and contexts.

CHRISTOPHER PRATT is one of Canada's most prominent painters and printmakers. Throughout his career, he has received many honours, including being named a Companion of the Order of Canada and receiving several honourary doctoral degrees. Pratt also designed the provincial flag of Newfoundland and Labrador, and has work included in major collections, both public and private, throughout Canada and other parts of the world. Retrospectives of his work have been organized by the Vancouver Art Gallery in 1985, and again in 2005 by the National Gallery of Canada. He continues, since 1963, to live and work in his studio in St. Mary's Bay.

ALSO BY CHRISTOPHER PRATT

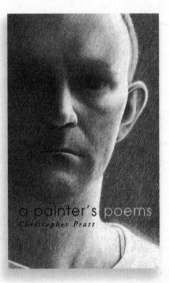

A Painter's Poems comprises poetry that Pratt has written over the past 50 years. They respond to encounters with people, places and events that have had an impact on his working life.

SPECIFICATIONS: 5 x 8 / 64 PP / $16.95 PB   ISBN-13: 978-1-55081-152-0

My poetry is a personal exorcism; I am aware that exorcism is not always 'art'. It is a self-portrait, random pages from a 'diary' in code, and portraits of others, friends, anonymous, given the protection of pronouns. I use simple language: some poetry glitters and illuminates like a foyer chandelier; I think mine as a single light bulb in a porch. – CHRISTOPHER PRATT, 1999